SO-AQL-479

S Hury
5/6/2004

The
Dynamics of Life

The Dynamics of Life

An Introduction to Dianetics Discoveries

L. Ron Hubbard

DIANETICS © LOS GATOS
475 ALBERTO WAY SUITE 110
LOS GATOS, CA 95032
(408) 354-1201

BRIDGE PUBLICATIONS, INC.

Published in the USA by
Bridge Publications, Inc.
1414 North Catalina Street
Los Angeles, California 90027-9990

ISBN 0-88404-101-8 Hardback
ISBN 0-88404-112-3 Trade Paperback

Published in all other countries by
New Era Publications ApS
Store Kongensgade 55
Copenhagen K, Denmark

ISBN 87-7336-209 9 Hardback
ISBN 87-7336-208 5 Trade Paperback

Copyright © 1983
By L. Ron Hubbard
All Rights Reserved

Dianetics™ *is a trademark and service mark*
owned by Religious Technology Center.

No part of this book may be reproduced or utilized in any
form or by any means electronic or mechanical, including
photocopying, recording or by any information storage and
retrieval system, without permission of the copyright owner.

Originally published as *Dianetics: The Original Thesis* copyright © 1951,
1967, 1970, 1973, 1976

This book is part of the works of L. Ron Hubbard, who
developed *Dianetics*™ spiritual healing technology. It is
presented to the reader as a record of observations and
research into the nature of the human mind and spirit, and
not as a statement of claims made by the author. The benefits
and goals of *Dianetics* can be attained only by the dedicated
efforts of the reader.

A Hubbard Electrometer, or *E-Meter*™ confessional aid, is a
device which is sometimes used in *Dianetics*. In itself, the
E-Meter does nothing. It is not intended or effective for the
diagnosis, treatment or prevention of any disease, or for the
improvement of health or any bodily function.

Book Design: Connie Gomberg

Printed in the United States of America

*D*ianetics™ spiritual healing technology is a precision subject that stems from the study and codification of survival. The word comes from the Greek *dia*—"through," and *nous*—"soul." It is further defined as what the soul is doing to the body.

Dianetics is pervasive. Human behavior and human thought are the foundation of human endeavor.[1] Once one has an answer to these basic riddles, there is almost nothing which will not eventually resolve.

---

1. endeavor: an earnest attempt or effort.

Contents

---

1. axioms: statements of natural laws on the order of those of the physical sciences.
2. dynamics: there could be said to be eight urges (drives, impulses) in life. These we call dynamics. These are motives or motivations.
3. engram: a mental image picture which is a recording of a time of physical pain and unconsciousness. It must by definition have impact or injury as part of its content.
4. aberration: a departure from rational thought or behavior.
5. tone scale: is essentially an assignation of numerical value by which individuals can be numerically classified. It is not arbitrary but will be found to approximate some actual governing law in nature.
6. dramatization: to repeat in action what has happened to one in experience. That's a basic definition of it, but much more important, it's a replay now of something that happened then. It's being replayed out of its time and period.
7. Auditor's Code: the governing set of rules for the general activity of auditing.

8. auditing: Dianetics auditing includes as its basic principle the exhaustion of all the painfully unconscious moments of a subject's life.

9. chain: a series of incidents of similar nature or similar subject matter.

10. returning: the person can "send" a portion of his mind to a past period on either a mental or combined mental and physical basis and can reexperience incidents which have taken place in his past in the same fashion and with the same sensations as before.

Foreword

You are about to begin the most exciting adventure of your life—the discovery of *self*.

What are your true potentials and capabilities?

It has been said that man uses only five to ten percent of his mental faculties. The full capabilities of the human mind have never been measured.

This book can help you to discover your full inherent potential with *Dianetics*™ spiritual healing technology.

Dianetics, derived from the Greek words *dia* (through) and *nous* (soul), is an exploration into the most fascinating realm on earth—the human mind and spirit.

The Dynamics of Life—An Introduction to Dianetics Discoveries is the first manuscript of Dianetics, written several years before the multimillion copy best seller, *Dianetics: The Modern Science of Mental Health*. As an unpublished manuscript, it enjoyed a wide grass-roots circulation among doctors, engineers and scientists throughout the United States. The original manuscript was eagerly copied and re-copied and passed from hand to hand.

Years of testing Dianetics techniques went into this first manuscript. Here, L. Ron Hubbard presented his discoveries and breakthroughs for the first time. The enthusiasm generated by this original manuscript eventually led to the publication of the popular workbook of Dianetics—*Dianetics: The Modern Science of Mental Health.*

The Dynamics of Life—An Introduction to Dianetics Discoveries is L. Ron Hubbard's concise introduction to the subject of Dianetics. Here, you'll discover the *reactive mind,* that part of your mind where all the physical and emotional pains you've ever suffered are stored. You'll learn how, when you least want it, this part of the mind can take control of you and make you *react* to life in ways you don't want to—like feeling afraid or angry or depressed.

Most importantly, you'll learn how to master the reactive mind. Underneath that reactive mind of yours is a strong, confident you and a *healthy* mind with near-infinite capabilities.

Millions of people all over the world have experienced the incredible benefits of Dianetics.

Your adventure begins on the following pages.

The Editors ☐

Important Note

In reading this book, be very certain you never go past a word you do not fully understand.

The only reason a person gives up a study or becomes confused or unable to learn is because he or she has gone past a word that was not understood.

The confusion or inability to grasp comes **after** a word was not understood.

Have you ever had the experience of coming to the end of a page and realizing that you didn't know what you had read? Somewhere earlier on that page you passed a word that you didn't understand.

Here's an example. "It was found that when the crepuscule arrived the children were quieter and when it was not present, they were much livelier." You see what happens. You think you don't understand the whole idea, but the inability to understand came entirely from the one word you could not define, *crepuscule*, which means twilight or darkness.

If, in reading this book, the materials become confusing or you can't seem to grasp it, there will be a word just earlier that you haven't understood. Don't go any further but go back to **before** you got into difficulty. Find the misunderstood word and get it defined.

Footnotes and Glossary

As an aid to the reader, words that are sometimes misunderstood have been defined in footnotes where they occur in the text. Words sometimes have several meanings. The footnote definitions given in this book only give the meaning that the word has as it is used in the text and the number of that definition in the dictionary. A glossary including all the footnoted definitions is included at the back of this book. Other definitions can be found in various dictionaries.

Introduction

In 1932 an investigation was undertaken to determine the dynamic[1] principle of existence[2] in a workable form which might lead to the resolution of some of the problems of mankind. A long research in ancient and modern philosophy[3] culminated, in 1938, in the heuristically[4] discovered primary law. A work was written at that time which embraced[5] man and his activities. In the following years further research was undertaken in order to prove or disprove the axioms[6] so established.

Certain experiences during the war made it necessary for the writer to resolve the work into applicable equations and an intensive program was begun in 1945 toward this end.

A year later many techniques had been discovered or evolved and a nebulous[7] form of the present work was formulated. Financed chiefly by a lump sum disability compensation, that form of Dianetics was intensively applied to volunteer subjects, and the work gradually developed to its present form.

Dianetics has been under test by the writer, as here delineated,[8] for the past three years. The last series of random volunteers, numbering twenty, were rehabilitated, twenty out of twenty,

---

1. dynamic: 1. relating to energy or physical force in motion.
2. dynamic principle of existence: is **Survive!** No behavior or activity has been found to exist without this principle. It is not new that life is surviving. It is new that life has as its entire dynamic urge only survival.
3. philosophy: 1. the rational investigation of the truths and principles of being, knowledge or conduct.
4. heuristic: 1. serving to find out; specifically applied to a system of education under which the student is trained to find out things for himself.
5. embrace: 5. to include; contain.
6. axioms: statements of natural laws on the order of those of the physical sciences.
7. nebulous: 3. unclear; vague; indefinite.
8. delineate: 3. to depict in words; describe.

with an average number of work hours of 151.2 per subject. Dianetics offers the first anatomy of the human mind and techniques for handling the hitherto[9] unknown reactive mind,[10] which causes irrational and psychosomatic[11] behavior. It has successfully removed any compulsions,[12] repressions,[13] neuroses[14] and psychoses[15] to which it has been applied.

L. R. H.
January, 1948

2

9.　hitherto: until this time.

10.　reactive mind: the portion of the mind which works on a stimulus-response basis (given a certain stimulus it will automatically give a certain response) which is not under a person's volitional [of or having to do with a person's own power of choice] control and which exerts force and power over a person's awareness, purposes, thoughts, body and actions.

11.　psychosomatic: psycho of course refers to mind and somatic refers to body; the term psychosomatic means the mind making the body ill or illnesses which have been created physically within the body by derangement of the mind.

12.　compulsion: 3. an irresistible, repeated, irrational impulse to perform some act.

13.　repression: a command that the organism must not do something.

14.　neurosis: an emotional state containing conflicts and emotional data inhibiting the abilities or welfare of the individual.

15.　psychosis: a conflict of commands which seriously reduce the individual's ability to solve his problems in his environment to a point where he cannot adjust some vital phase of his environmental needs.

CHAPTER ONE

Primary Axioms

Dianetics is a heuristic science built upon axioms. Workability rather than idealism[1] has been consulted. The only claim made for these axioms is that by their use certain definite and predictable results can be obtained.

3

The principal achievement of Dianetics lies in its organization. Almost any of its parts can be found somewhere in history, even when they were independently evolved by the writer. There are no principal sources, and where a practice or a principle is borrowed from some past school[2] the connection is usually accidental and does not admit any further use or validity of that school. Dianetics will work, and can only be worked, when regarded and used as a unity. When diluted by broader applications of older practices, it will no longer produce results. To avoid confusion and prevent semantic[3] difficulties, new and simplified terminology has been used and is used only as defined herein.

Dianetics is actually a family of sciences. It is here addressed in the form of a science of thought applicable to psychosomatic ills and individual aberrations.[4]

The field of thought may be divided into two areas which have been classified as the "knowable" and the "unknowable." We are here concerned only with the "knowable." In the "unknowable" we place that data which we do not need to know in order to solve

---

1.   idealism: 1. behavior or thought based on a conception of things as they should be or as one would wish them to be.
2.   school: 8a. a group of people held together by the same teachings, beliefs, opinions, methods, etc.
3.   semantic: 1. of or pertaining to meaning, especially meaning in language.
4.   aberration: a departure from rational thought or behavior.

the problem of improving or resolving aberrations of the human mind. By thus splitting the broad field of thought, we need not now concern ourselves with such indefinites as spiritualism, deism,[5] telepathy,[6] clairvoyance[7] or, for instance, the human soul.

Conceiving this split as a line drawn through the area, we can assign a dynamic principle of existence to all that data remaining in the "knowable" field.

After exhaustive research one word was selected as embracing the finite universe as a dynamic principle of existence. This word can be used as a guide or a measuring stick and by it can be evaluated much information. It is therefore our first and our controlling axiom.

The first axiom is:

Survive!

This can be seen to be the lowest common denominator[8] of the finite universe. It embraces all forms of energy. It further delineates the purpose of that energy so far as it is now viewable by us in the "knowable" field. The activity of the finite universe can easily be seen to obey this axiom as though it were a command. All works and energies can be considered to be motivated by it. The various kingdoms[9] have this as their lowest common denominator, for animals, vegetables and minerals are all striving for survival. We do not know to what end we are surviving, and in our field of the "knowable" and in our choice of only the workable axioms, we do not know and have no immediate reason to ask why.

All forms of energy are then surviving to some unknown end, for some unknown purpose. We need only to know that they *are* surviving and that, as units or species, they *must* survive.

---

5.   deism: belief in the existence of a God on purely rational grounds without reliance on revelation or authority; especially, the 17th and 18th century doctrine that God created the world and its natural laws, but takes no further part in its functioning.

6.   telepathy: communication from one mind to another without the use of speech or writing or gestures, etc.

7.   clairvoyance: 1. the supposed ability to perceive things that are not in sight or that cannot be seen.

8.   common denominator: 2. a trait, characteristic, belief or the like, common to or shared by all members of a group.

9.   kingdom: 3. any of the three great divisions into which all natural objects have been classified (the animal, vegetable and mineral kingdoms).

By derivation from the first workable axiom, we come into possession of the second. In obedience to the command *survive,* life took on the form of a cell which, joining with other cells, formed a colony. The cell, by procreating,[10] expanded the colony. The colony, by procreation, formed other colonies. Colonies of different types united and necessity, mutation[11] and natural selection[12] brought about specializing which increased the complexity of the colonies until they became an aggregation.[13] The problems of the colonial aggregation were those of food, protection and procreation. In various ways a colonial aggregation of cells became a standardized unity and any advanced colonial aggregation came into possession by necessity, mutation and natural selection of a central control system.

5

The purpose of the colonial aggregation was to survive. To do this it had to have food, means of defense, protection and means of procreation. The control center which had developed had as its primary command, *survive!* Its prime purpose was the food, defense, protection and means of procreation.

Thus can be stated the second workable axiom:

The purpose of the mind[14] is to solve problems relating to survival.

The ultimate success of the organism, its species or life would be, at its unimaginable extreme, immortality. The final failure in obedience to the law *survive* would be death. Between eternal survival and death lie innumerable gradations. In the middle ground of such a scale would be mere existence without hope of much success and without fear of failure. Below this point would lie, step by step, innumerable small errors, accidents, losses, each one of which would tend to abbreviate[15] the chances of reaching the ultimate goal. Above this point would lie the small successes, appreciations and triumphs which would tend to secure the desirable goal.

---

10. procreate: to bring (a living thing) into existence by the natural process of reproduction, to generate.
11. mutation: 1. change or alteration in form.
12. natural selection: a process in nature resulting in the survival and perpetuation of only those forms of plant and animal life having certain favorable characteristics that best enable them to adapt to a specific environment.
13. aggregation: 2. collection into an unorganized whole.
14. mind: is the command post of operation and is constructed to resolve problems and pose problems related to survival and only to survival.
15. abbreviate: to shorten by cutting off a part; to cut short.

As an axiom, the mind can then be said to act in obedience to a central basic command, *survive,* and to direct or manage the organism in its efforts to accomplish the ultimate goal for the individual or species or life, and to avoid for the individual or species or life any part of the final failure, which leads to the stated axiom:

The mind directs the organism, the species, its symbiotes[16] or life in the effort of survival.

A study of the field of evolution will indicate that survival has been, will be and is the sole test of an organism, whether the organism is treated in the form of a daily activity or the life of the species. No action of the organism will be found to lie without the field of survival, for the organism is acting within its environment upon information received or recorded, and error or failure does not alter the fact that its basic impulse was motivated by survival.

Another axiom may then be formulated as follows:

The mind as the central direction system of the body, poses,[17] perceives and resolves problems of survival and directs or fails to direct their execution.

As there are many organisms in the same species, all attempting to accomplish the same end, and as there are many species, and as matter itself is attempting in one unit form or another to survive, there is necessarily conflict and contest amongst the individuals of the species, species or units of matter. Species cannot survive without being interested primarily in the species. Natural selection and other causes have established this as a primary rule for survival: *That the unit remain alive as long as possible as a unit and, by association and procreation, that the species remain alive as a species.* Second-grade interest is paid by the unit or the species to its symbiotes. Third-grade interest is paid to inanimate[18] matter. As this is apparently the most workable solution, natural selection best preserves those species which follow this working rule. And the

---

16. symbiotes: the Dianetics meaning of symbiote is extended beyond the dictionary definition to mean "any or all life or energy forms which are mutually dependent for survival." The atom depends on the universe, the universe on the atom.

17. pose: 4. to put forward, to present.

18. inanimate: 1. (of rocks and other objects) lifeless, (of plants) lacking animal life.

symbiotes of the successful species therefore have enhanced opportunity for survival.

Man is the most successful organism currently in existence, at least on this planet. Man is currently winning in the perpetual cosmic[19] election which possibly may select the thinker of the new **Thought.**

Man is heir to the experience and construction of his own ancestors. As cellular conservatism is one of the factors of survival, his brain is basically the same brain which directed and resolved the problems of his animal forebears.[20] By evolution and natural selection, this brain therefore has the primary priority in emergencies. Superimposed[21] on this animal brain has been developed an enormously complex analyzer, which probably exists in his frontal lobe.[22]

7

The command, *survive,* is variable in individuals and species to the extent that it may be strong or weak. Superior strength of the command in the individual or species is normally, but variably, a survival factor. The primary facet[23] of personality is the basic strength of the *dynamic* drive.

The *dynamic* is variable from individual to individual and race to race. It is varied by physiology, environment and experience. Its manifestation in the animal brain affects the tenacity[24] of the individual to life or purpose, and it affects the activity of the analyzer. The first characteristic of the individual which should be considered is the basic strength of his *dynamic*. By this an axiom can be formulated:

The persistency of the individual in life is directly governed by the strength of his basic dynamic.

The analytical, human or, as it has elsewhere been called erroneously, the conscious mind, is variable from individual to

---

19.   cosmic: 1. of the universe.
20.   forebear: an ancestor.
21.   superimpose: to lay or place (a thing) on top of something else.
22.   frontal lobe: 1. portion of the brain behind the forehead.
23.   facet: 2. any of a number of sides or aspects, as of a personality.
24.   tenacity: the quality or state of being tenacious (5. persistent; stubborn).

individual and race to race in its ability to perceive and resolve problems. Another axiom can then be formulated:

Intelligence is the ability of an individual, group or race to resolve problems relating to survival.

It should be noted that there is a distinct difference between the *dynamic* and the intelligence. High intelligence may not denote[25] high *dynamic*. High *dynamic* may not denote high intelligence. *Intelligence* is mental sensitivity and analytical ability. *Dynamic* is the persistency of the individual in obedience to the command, *survive!*

It has been noted that there is a gradation in the scale of survival. Gains toward the ultimate goal are pleasurable. Failures toward the final defeat are sorrowful or painful. Pleasure is therefore the perception of well-being, or an advance toward the ultimate goal. Pain, therefore, is the perception of a reduction toward the final defeat. Both are necessary survival factors.

For the purpose of Dianetics, *good* and *evil* must be defined. Those things which may be classified as *good* by an individual are only those things which aid himself, his family, his group, his race, mankind or life in its dynamic obedience to the command, modified by the observations of the individual, his family, his group, his race or life.

As *evil* may be classified those things which tend to limit the dynamic thrust of the individual, his family, his group, his race or life in general in the dynamic drive, also limited by the observation, the observer and his ability to observe.

Good may be defined as constructive. *Evil* may be defined as destructive—definitions modified by viewpoint. The individual man is an organism attempting to survive in affinity or contest with other men, races and the three kingdoms. His goal is survival for himself, his progeny,[26] his group, his race, his symbiotes, life and the

8

---

25.   denote: 1. be a sign of; indicate.
26.   progeny: children, descendents or offspring collectively.

universe in general in contest with any efforts or entities which threaten or impede his efforts to attain the goal.

His happiness depends upon making, consolidating[27] or contemplating gains toward his goal.

It is a purpose of Dianetics to pass man across the abyss[28] of irrational, solely reactive thought[29] and enter him upon a new stage of constructive progression to the ultimate goal. □

---

27. consolidate: 2. to make or become strong, stable, firmly established, etc.
28. abyss: 2. anything too deep for measurement; profound depth.
29. reactive thought: the reactive mind is distinguished by the fact that although it thinks, it thinks wholly in identities. For instance, to the reactive mind under certain conditions there would be no difference between a microphone and a table.

CHAPTER TWO

An Analogy[1] of the Mind

It is not the purpose of Dianetics to reconstruct the human mind. The purpose of Dianetics is to delete from the existing mind those physically painful experiences which have resulted in the aberration of the analytical mind, to resolve the physical manifestations[2] of mental aberration, and to restore in its entirety the proper working function of a brain not otherwise physically deranged.[3]

Dianetics thus *embraces* the various aspects of psychosomatic conditions, including the glandular[4] balance or imbalance of the organism, as influenced by painful physical experience. However, its purpose is not one of healing, and its address is not to such psychosomatic manifestations specifically, but rather to those aberrative experiences in which these conditions have their roots.

The initial adjustments of the individual are included in Child Dianetics[5] and Educational Dianetics.[6] Judicial Dianetics,[7] Political Dianetics[8] and Military Dianetics are elsewhere touched upon or allocated for study. Dianetics, as a family of sciences, proceeds

---

1.   analogy: 2. an explaining of something by comparing it point by point with something similar.
2.   manifestation: 2. something that manifests or is manifested (1. to make clear or evident; show plainly; reveal).
3.   derange: 1. to upset the arrangement, order or operation of; unsettle; disorder.
4.   glandular: 3. derived from or affected by glands [organs that secrete substances to be used in other parts of the body or expelled from it].
5.   Child Dianetics: that branch of Dianetics which is concerned with promoting optimum survival of the immature human organism until such time as standard procedure for adults may be employed.
6.   Educational Dianetics: contains the body of organized knowledge necessary to train minds to their optimum efficiency and to an optimum of skill and knowledge in the various branches of the works of man.
7.   Judicial Dianetics: covers the field of adjudication within the society and amongst the societies of man. Of necessity it embraces jurisprudence [science or philosophy of law] and its codes and establishes precision definitions and equations for the establishment of equity. It is the science of judgment.
8.   Political Dianetics: embraces the field of group activity and organization to establish the optimum conditions and processes of leadership and intergroup relations.

however from the axioms cursorily[9] touched upon in the last chapter and is uniformly governed by the principles of the behavior of the human mind.

When an individual is acting contrary to survival of himself, his group, progeny, race, mankind or life he can be considered to be unintelligent, uninformed or aberrated. *Every single instance of aberrated conduct threatening the general goal of the individual as outlined in the last chapter can be proven to have a source which will specifically be found to be a painful experience containing data not available to the analytical mind.* Every single instance and facet of aberrated conduct has its exact causation in the physically painful error which has been introduced during a moment of absence of the analytical power.

Dianetics consists of discovering the aberration in the individual, finding the physically painful experience which corresponds to it and placing the data therein contained at the disposal of the analytical mind.

More as effort to demonstrate how that is accomplished than as an actual outline of the character of the mind, the following analogy is offered.

First there is the physio-[10]animal section of the brain, containing the motor controls, the subbrains[11] and the physical nervous system in general, including the physical aspect of the analytical section of the brain. The control of all voluntary and involuntary muscles is contained in this section. It commands all body fluids, blood flow, respiration, glandular secretion, cellular construction and the activity of various parts of the body. Experimentation has adequately demonstrated this. The physio-animal mind has specific methods of "thinking." These are entirely reactive. Animal experimentation—rats, dogs, etc.—is experimentation on and with precisely this mind and little more. *It is a fully conscious mind and should never be denoted by any term which denies it "consciousness" since there is no period in the life of the organism from conception to death when this mind is not awake, observing and recording perceptics.*

---

9. cursory: hastily, often superficially, done; performed rapidly with little attention to detail.
10. physio: (a combining form meaning) 2. physical.
11. subbrains: there is a subbrain in various parts of the body . . . such parts of the body as the "funny bones" or any "judo sensitive" spots: the sides of the neck, the inside of the wrist, the places the doctors tap to find out if there is a reflex.

This is the mind of a dog, cat or rat and is also the basic mind of a man so far as its operating characteristics are concerned. A man in the deepest possible somnambulistic[12] sleep is still in possession of more mind and thinking and coordinating ability than a lower animal.

The term *consciousness* is no more than a designation of the awareness of *now*. The physio-animal mind never ceases to be aware of *now* and never ceases to record the successive instances of *now* which in their composite make up a *time track*[13] connecting memory in an orderly chain.

13

Cessation of life alone discontinues the recording of perceptions on this orderly track. *Unconsciousness* is a condition wherein the organism is discoordinated only in its analytical process and motor control direction. In the physio-animal section of the brain, a complete time track and a complete memory record of all perceptions for all moments of the organism's existence is available.

As life progresses, for instance, from a blade of grass, greater and greater complexities and degrees of self-determinism[14] are possible. Energy in its various forms is the primary motivator in the lower orders, but as the complexity of the order is increased into the animal kingdom, the physio-animal brain attains more and more command of the entire organism until it itself begins to possess the second section of the mind.

All animals possess in some slight degree an analyzer. This, which we designate the *analytical mind,* is present even in lower orders, since it is only that section of the brain which possesses the self-deterministic coordinative command of the physio-animal brain and thus of the body. In a rat, for instance, it is no more than its "conscious" awareness of *now* applying to lessons of *then* without rationality but with instinct[15] and painful experience. This is the analytical section of the mind in a lower animal but it is the *reactive*

---

12. somnambulism: the trancelike state of one who somnambulates (to get up and move about in a trancelike state while asleep).
13. time track: consists of all the consecutive moments of "now" from the earliest moment of life of the organism to present time.
14. self-determinism: means the ability to direct oneself.
15. instinct: 1. an inborn impulse or tendency to perform certain acts or behave in certain ways.

mind in a man whose *analytical mind* is so highly attuned[16] and intricate that it can command entirely the physio-animal brain and thus the body.

Man not only possesses a superior physio-animal mind but possesses as well an *analytical mind* of such power and complexity that it has no real rival in any other species. The *analytical mind* of man cannot be studied by observing the reactions of animals under any situations. Not only is it more sensitive but it possesses factors and sensitivities not elsewhere found.

14

Continuing this analogy: Lying between the *analytical mind* and the physio-animal mind may be conceived the *reactive mind*. This is the coordinated responses of the physio-animal mind, the "analytical" mind of animals, and the first post of emergency command in man. All errors of a psychic[17] or psychosomatic nature can be considered for the purposes of this analogy to lie in the *reactive mind*. The first human *analytical mind* took command of the body and physio-animal mind under strained and dangerous circumstances when man was still in violent contest with other species around him. It can be considered that the *analytical mind* received command with the single proviso[18] that instantaneous emergency would be handled by the outdated but faster *reactive mind*.

Any and all errors in thinking and action derive from the reactive mind as it is increased in strength and power by painful experience. It can be called a shadow mind, instantaneously reactive when any of its content is perceived in the environment of the individual, at which time it urgently bypasses the analytical mind and causes immediate reaction in the physio-animal mind and in the body. Additionally, the reactive mind is in continual presence when chronically restimulated by a constantly present restimulator—which is to say, an approximation[19] of the reactive mind's content or some part thereof continually perceived in the environment of the organism. The reactive mind is in action so long as it is activated by an exact or nearly exact approximation of its content. But given too

---

16.   attune: to adjust; bring into accord, harmony or sympathetic relationship.
17.   psychic: 1. of or having to do with the psyche [soul] or mind.
18.   proviso: 2. a condition or stipulation.
19.   approximation: 3. a coming or getting near to identity in quantity, quality or degree; an approach to a correct estimate or conception of anything.

continuous a restimulation, it can and does derange both the physio-animal mind and body below it and the analytical mind above it. It was created by deranging circumstances of a physical nature, hence it deranges.

The entire content of the reactive mind is records of physical pain with its accompanying perceptions during disconnection of the analyzer. All aberrated conduct and error on the part of an individual is occasioned[20] by restimulation of his reactive mind.

None of these minds are "unconscious," nor are they subconscious. The entire organism is always conscious but the temporary dispersion[21] of the thought processes of the analytical mind brings about a condition whereby that mind, having been dispersed and considering itself the residence of the person, is unable to obtain and reach data perceived and received by the organism during the analytical mind's condition of dispersion. That the analytical mind can be thrown, by pain or shock, out of circuit is a survival factor of its own: as sensitive "machinery" it must be protected by a fuse system. □

15

20.   occasion: to cause.
21.   disperse: to scatter, to go or drive or send in different directions.

CHAPTER THREE

The Dynamics

The basic dynamic, **survive**, increases in complexity as the complexity of the organism evolves. Energy may be considered to have taken many paths through eternity to arrive intact at the infinite goal. The "why" of the goal may lie above the finite line but below it, demarked by the word *survive,* definite manifestations are visible. Energy collects into various forms of matter which collect and aggregate in various materials and compounds. Life evolves from the simplest basic into complex forms since evolutionary change is in itself a method of survival.

Conflict amongst species and individuals within the species is additionally a survival factor. Affinity of individuals for groups, races and the whole of its species, and for other species, is additionally a survival factor, as strong or stronger than conflict.

Drive is defined as the dynamic thrust through time toward the attainment of the goal. Survive is considered to be the lowest common denominator of all energy efforts and all forms. It can then be subdivided specifically into several drive lines as applicable to each form or species. The unaberrated self contains eight main drives which are held in common with man.

The dynamics are: One, self; Two, sex; Three, group; Four, mankind; Five, life; Six, the physical universe; Seven, thought; Eight, universal thought or infinity.

An entire philosophy can be built around each one of these dynamics which will account for all the actions of an individual. Any one of these philosophies is so complete that it can be logically made

17

to include the other seven. In other words, all purpose of an individual can be rationalized[1] into the dynamic of self. A philosophy exists which attempts to rationalize everything into the sexual dynamic, and so on with all the dynamics. Observing that each one can stand as a logical unity, one finds it necessary to retire[2] to the lowest common denominator of the basic dynamic which actually does explain the eight subdivisions. As each one of the subdivisions is capable of supporting the whole weight[3] of a rational argument, it can readily be deduced that each is of nearly equal importance in the individual. The aberrated conditions of a society tend to vary the stress on these dynamics, making first one and then another the keynote[4] of the society.

18

In an unaberrated individual or society, the validity of all eight would be recognized.

The unaberrated individual may physiologically[5] possess or environmentally stress one or more of these dynamics above the others. In terms of basic personality, the physiological-environmental-educational aspect of the individual is of varied strength in the eight dynamics.

Each one of the eight dynamics breaks further into purposes which are specific and complex. Purposes and other factors entangle these dynamics, and varying situations and the observational power of the individual may conflict one of these dynamics against another within the individual himself. This is a basic complex factor of unaberrated personality.

I. **The Dynamic of Self** consists of the dynamic thrust to survive as an individual, to obtain pleasure as an individual and to avoid pain. It covers the general field of food, clothing and shelter, personal ambition and general individual purpose.

II. **The Dynamic of Sex** embraces the procreation of

---

1. rationalize: 2. to explain or interpret on rational grounds.
2. retire: 4. to return; to come back.
3. weight: 8. influence, power or authority.
4. keynote: 2. the basic idea or ruling principle, as of a speech, policy, etc.
5. physiological: 1. of or pertaining to physiology (2. the organic processes or functions of an organism or any of its parts).

progeny, the care of that progeny and the securing for that progeny of better survival conditions and abilities in the future.

III. **The Dynamic of Group** embraces the various units of the species of man, such as the association, the military company,[6] the people in the surrounding countryside, the nation and the race. It is characterized by activity on the part of the individual to obtain and maintain the survival of the group of which he is a part.

IV. **The Mankind Dynamic** embraces the survival of the species.

V. **The Dynamic of Life** is the urge of the individual to survive for life and for life to survive for itself.

VI. **The Physical Universe Dynamic** is the drive of the individual to enhance the survival of all matter, energy, time and space.

VII. **The Thought Dynamic** concerns the urge of the individual to survive as thought.

VIII. **The Dynamic of Universal Thought** is the urge of the individual to survive for the Creator.

While man is concerned with any one of the above dynamics, any one of them may become antipathetic[7] to his own survival. This is *rational conflict* and is normally and commonly incidental to survival. It is nonaberrative in that it is rational within the educational limitation.

The family as a unit is not a dynamic but a combination of dynamics. And in this and other societies it attains a position of interest which is not necessarily inherent in the individual or group.

Basically simple, complexity is introduced amongst the dynamics by individual and group irrationalities. The basic (unaberrated) individual has continual difficulty rationalizing the problems

19

---

6.   company (military): 9b. any relatively small group of soldiers.
7.   antipathetic: 2. opposed or antagonistic in character, tendency, etc.

of importances and choices amongst these dynamics. When the basic individual becomes aberrated and is attendantly[8] unable to reason freely on all problems, a selection of importances amongst these dynamics becomes nearly impossible and produces aberrated solutions which may resolve[9] such an extreme as the destruction of the individual himself, by himself, under the mistaken solution that he may thus obey the primary command.

Note: All self-destructive effort is irrationality of a precise nature which will often be found by the auditor[10] in his preclear[11] during auditing[12] but which forms no part of the basic personality of that individual.   □

20

---

8.   attendant: 3. accompanying as a circumstance or result.
9.   resolve: 14. to determine or decide upon (a course of action, etc.).
10.   auditor: the individual who administers Dianetics procedures. To audit means "to listen" and also "to compute."
11.   preclear: any person who has been entered into Dianetics processing.
12.   auditing: the application of Dianetics processes and procedures to someone by a trained auditor. Dianetics auditing includes as its basic principle the exhaustion of all the painfully unconscious moments of a subject's life.

CHAPTER FOUR

The Basic Individual

For the purposes of this work the terms *basic individual* and *Clear* are nearly synonymous since they denote the unaberrated self in complete integration[1] and in a state of highest possible rationality; a *Clear* is one who has become the *basic individual* through auditing.

21

The precise personality of the basic individual is of interest to the auditor. His complete characteristic is established by:

(1) the strength of his basic *dynamic;* (2) the relative strengths of his dynamics; (3) the sensitivity, which is to say the intelligence, of his analyzer; (4) the coordination of his motor controls; (5) his physiological and glandular condition; (6) his environment and education.

The experiences of each individual also create an individual composite and so may additionally designate individuality. There are as many distinct individuals on earth as there are men, women and children. That we can establish a common denominator of drive and basic function does not, cannot and will not alter the fact that individuals are amazingly varied one from the next.

It will be found by experience and exhaustive research, as it has been clinically established, that the basic individual is invariably responsive in all the dynamics and is essentially "good." There are varying degrees of courage but in the basic individual there is no pusillanimity.[2] The virtues[3] of the basic individual are

---

1. integration: 3. the organization of various traits, feelings, attitudes, etc., into one harmonious personality.
2. pusillanimity: lacking courage; cowardly.
3. virtue: 1. moral excellence, goodness, a particular form of this.

innumerable. His intentional vices[4] and destructive dramatizations[5] are nonexistent. He is in close alignment with that ideal which mankind recognizes as an ideal. This is a necessary part of an auditor's working knowledge, since deviations from it denote the existence of aberration, and such departures are unnatural and enforced and are no part of the self-determinism of the individual.

Man is not a reactive animal. He is capable of self-determinism. He has willpower. He ordinarily has high analytical ability. He is rational and he is happy and integrated only when he is his own basic personality.

22

The most desirable state in an individual is complete self-determinism. Such self-determinism may be altered and shaped to some degree by education and environment, but so long as the individual is not aberrated, he is in possession of self-determinism. So long as he is self-determined in his actions he adjusts himself successfully to the degree that his environment will permit such an adjustment. He will be more forceful, effective and happier in that environment than when aberrated.

That the basic personality is "good" does not mean that he cannot be a terribly effective enemy of those things rationally recognizable as destructive to himself and to his.

The basic individual is not a buried unknown or a different person, but an intensity of all that is best and most able in the person. The basic individual equals the same person minus his pain and dramatizations.

The drive strength of the person does not derive from his aberrations. The aberrations lessen the drive strength. Artistry, personal force, personality, all are residual in the basic personality. This is derived from clinical research and experimentation. The only reason an aberree[6] occasionally holds hard to his aberrations is due to the fact that his engrams[7] have a content which forbids their removal.

☐

---

4. vice: 1a. an evil or wicked action, habit or characteristic.
5. dramatization: to repeat in action what has happened to one in experience. That's a basic definition of it, but much more important, it's a replay now of something that happened then. It's being replayed out of its time and period.
6. aberree: an aberrated person.
7. engram: a mental image picture which is a recording of a time of physical pain and unconsciousness. It must by definition have impact or injury as part of its content.

CHAPTER FIVE

Engrams

The reactive mind consists of a collection of experiences   23
received during an unanalytical moment which contain pain and
actual or conceived antagonism to the survival of the individual. An
engram is a perceptic entity which can be precisely defined. The
aggregate of engrams compose the reactive mind.

A new subfield entitled "Perceptics"[1] has been originated
here to define adequately engramic data. Perceptics contains as one
of its facets the field of semantics.[2] Precisely as the field of semantics
is organized so is organized, in Perceptics, each sensory perception.

The audio-[3]syllabic[4] communication system of man has its
counterpart in various languages observable in lower animals. Words
are sounds in syllabic form delivered with a definite timbre,[5] pitch[6]
and volume or sight recognition in each case. Words are a highly
specialized form of audio-perceptics. The quality of the sound in
uttering the word is nearly as important as the word itself. The
written word belongs in part to visio-[7]perceptics. Having but lately
acquired his extensive vocabulary, the mind of man is least adjusted
to words and their sense. The mind is better able to differentiate
amongst qualities of utterance than amongst the meanings of words
themselves.

---

1. perceptics: sense messages.
2. semantics: 1a. the study of meaning.
3. audio: of hearing or sound.
4. syllabic: 1. of a syllable or syllables.
5. timbre: the characteristic quality of sound that distinguishes one voice or musical instrument from another or one vowel sound from another: it is determined by the harmonics of the sound and is distinguished from the intensity and pitch.
6. pitch: 16a. that quality of a tone or sound determined by the frequency of vibration of the sound waves reaching the ear: the greater the frequency, the higher the pitch.
7. visio: with visio we perceive light waves, which, as sight, are compared with experience and evaluated.

Included in perceptics in the same fashion and on the same axioms as semantics are the other sensory perceptions—organic sensation, the tactile[8] sense, the olfactory[9] sense and the senses involved with sight and hearing. Each has its own grouping. And each carries its class of messages with highly complex meanings. Each one of these divisions of the senses is plotted in time according to the earliest or most forceful significances. Each class of messages is so filed as to lead the individual toward pleasure and away from pain. The classifications and study of this varied sensory file has been designated "Perceptics."

24

Engrams are received into the mind forming a reactive area during moments of lowered analytical awareness of the individual, and they contain physical pain and antagonism to survival. The engram is a packaged perceptic not available to the analytical mind but intimately connected to the physio-animal mind. Under normal conditions it reacts as a dramatization of itself when approximated by the organism's perceptions of its content in the immediate environment during periods of weariness, illness or hypnotic[10] moments in the life of the individual.

When injury or illness supplants[11] the analytical mind producing what is commonly known as "unconsciousness" and when physical pain and antagonism to the survival of the organism are present, an engram is received by the individual. Subsequently, during moments when the potential of the analytical mind is reduced by weariness, illness or similar circumstances, one or more of the perceptics contained in the engram may be observed by the individual in his environment, and without his perceiving that he has observed it (or the identity of it) the individual dramatizes the moment of receipt of the engram.

An engram impedes one or more dynamics of the basic individual. Being antagonistic to his survival it can be considered analogically to consist of a reverse charge.[12]

---

8.   tactile: 2. of, having or related to the sense of touch.
9.   olfactory: 1. of or pertaining to the sense of smell.
10.   hypnotic: tending to produce sleep or a trance.
11.   supplant: 1. to take the place of; supercede, especially through force or plotting.
12.   charge: 39a. electrical charge, the quantity of electricity or electrical energy in or upon an object or substance.

As an example, the analytical mind can be said to possess multiple scanners in layers. Ordinary or pleasurable memory can be considered to have, as an analogy only, a positive charge. The multiple scanners are able to sweep these areas and make available memory data to the analytical mind so that it can arrive by various mathematical means at a solution for its various problems.

The engram, as a specific memory package, can be considered to have a reverse charge which cannot be reached by the scanner of the analytical mind but which is directly connected to the motor controls and other physical functions and which can exert, at a depth not nearly as basic as the basic drive but nevertheless low, a hidden influence upon the analytical mind through another circuit. The analytical mind in awareness of *now*, nevertheless, is unable to discover, without assistance from an auditor, the existence of such an impediment[13] since it was received during a moment of extremely low potential on the part of the analytical mind.

25

As a further analogy, and for demonstration only, an engram can be considered to be a bundle of perceptions of a precise nature. An engram is an entire dramatic sequence, implanted[14] during unconsciousness, which possesses specific perceptic keys,[15] any one of which, when unanalytically perceived by the individual in his environment, may in greater or lesser degrees set the engram into reaction.

Denied to the analytical mind at its reception, it is denied to the analytical mind in its exact character during its dramatization. Its content is literal and, on the physio-animal level, demands action. Man's analytical ability and his vocabulary are imposed above both the physio-animal mind and the reactive mind, both on the evolutionary time track and in awareness. The charge contained in the engram is inexhaustible and remains reactive in full force whenever keyed into the circuit by restimulators.

Restimulators are those approximations in the environment of an individual of the content of an engram. Restimulators can exist in any of the various senses. The orderly filing of perceptics

---

13. impediment: early term which meant the same as engram.
14. implant: 1. to plant firmly or deeply, embed.
15. key: 6. something that secures or controls entrance to a place.

in the memory does not, apparently, include the content of engrams, these being filed separately under an "immediate danger" heading.

There are three kinds of thought: the first is *engramic,* or *literal.* It demands immediate action without examination by the analytical mind. A hand being withdrawn from a hot stove when burned is being governed by the reactive principle, but as the ensuing instant of unconsciousness caused by the shock is ordinarily slight, no real engram can be said to have formed.

26   The second type of thought is *justified thought.* Engramic thought is literal, without reason, irrational. Justified thought is the attempt of the analytical mind to explain the reactive, engramic reactions of the organism in the ordinary course of living. Every engram may cause some form of aberrated conduct on the part of the individual. Justified thought is the effort of the conscious mind to explain away that aberration without admitting, as it cannot do normally, that it has failed the organism.

The third and optimum type of thought is *rational thought.* This is the thought used by a Clear.

An engram is an apparent surcharge[16] in the mental circuit with certain definite finite content. That charge is not reached or examined by the analytical mind, but that charge is capable of acting as an independent command.

When the basic drive of the individual is boosted in potential by an observed necessity, the residual charge in an engram is insufficient to contest, at times, the raised purpose. The analytical mind can then be seen to function in entire command of the organism without serious modification by engramic command.

At other times, hostility in the environment and confusion of the analytical mind combine to reduce the dynamic potential to such a degree that the engramic command, in comparison to the basic drive, can be seen to be extremely powerful. It is at such times,

---

16.   surcharge: 1b. an overcharge.

in the presence of even faint restimulators, that the individual most demonstrates his aberrations.

Example: Engram received at the age of 3½ years. Adult preclear. As child in dental chair, against his will, under antagonistic conditions, given nitrous oxide[17] and tricked by dentist. During painful portion of treatment the dentist says, "He is asleep. He can't hear, feel or see anything. Stay there."

The perceptics which can be restimulated in this are the quality, pitch and volume of the dentist's voice; the sound of the dentist's drill; the slap of the cable running the drill; street noises of a specific kind; the tactile of the mouth being forcibly held open; the smell of the mask; the sound of running water; the smell of nitrous oxide; and in short, several of each perceptic class, excluding only sight.

The effect of this experience, being a part of an engramic chain[18] which contained two earlier experiences, was in some small degree to trance[19] the individual and maintain some portion of him in a regressed[20] state.

This engram is too brief and extraordinarily simple but it will serve as an example to the auditor. The timeless quality of the suggestions, the conceived antagonism, precursors[21] on the engramic chain awakened and reinforced, all these things confused the time sense of the individual and were otherwise reactive[22] in later life.

For every engram there is a somatic[23] as part of that engram. No aberration exists without its somatics unless it is a racial-educational aberration, in which instance it is compatible with its environment and so is not considered irrational.

---

17. nitrous oxide: a colorless, nonflammable gas . . . used as an anesthetic and in aerosols.
18. chain: a series of incidents of similar nature or similar subject matter.
19. trance: 6. to put in a trance (1. a half-conscious state, seemingly between sleeping and waking, in which ability to function voluntarily may be suspended).
20. regress: 1. to go back; return; move backward.
21. precursor: earlier engram.
22. reactive: irrational, reacting instead of acting.
23. somatic: body sensation, illness or pain or discomfort. "Soma" means body. Hence psychosomatic or pains stemming from the mind.

Every aberration contains its exact command in some engram.

The numbers of engrams per individual are relatively few. The aberrated condition of the individual does not depend on the number of engrams but the severity of individual engrams.

An engram is severe in the exact ratio that it is conceived by the organism to have been a moment of threat to survival. The character of the threat and the perceptic content produce the aberration. A number of engrams with similar perceptics in an individual produce a complex aberration pattern which nevertheless has for its parts individual engrams.

An aberration is the manifestation of an engram and is serious only when it influences the competence of the individual in his environment.

Engrams are of two types depending upon the duration of restimulation. There are *floaters* and *chronics*. A floater has not been restimulated in the individual during the lifetime succeeding it. A chronic is an engram which has been more or less continuously restimulated so that it has become an apparent portion of the individual. A chronic begins to gather "locks."[24] A floater has not accumulated locks since it has never been restimulated.

A lock can be conceived to be joined to an engram in such a way that it can be reached by the multiple scanners of the analytical mind which cannot reach the engram. A lock is a painful mental experience. It is or is not regarded by the analytical mind as a source of difficulty or aberration. It is a period of mental anguish and is wholly dependent upon an engram for its pain value. When an engram is activated into a chronic, it accumulates numerous locks along the time track of the individual. The engram itself is not immediately locatable, except somatically, along the time track of the individual. Locks are of some diagnostic[25] value but, as they exist as

24.   lock: an analytical moment in which the perceptics of the engram are approximated, thus restimulating the engram or bringing it into action, the present-time perceptics being erroneously interpreted by the reactive mind to mean that the same condition which produced physical pain once before is now again at hand.

25.   diagnostic: 1. of or constituting a diagnosis (2. a careful examination and analysis of the facts in an attempt to understand or explain something).

experiences more or less recallable by the analytical mind, they can be depended upon to vanish upon the removal of the engram from the reactive mind.

The running of a lock as a lock has some value but the exhaustion[26] of locks from an aberrated individual is long and arduous and is seldom productive of any lasting result. Upon the location and exhaustion of the engram from the reactive mind, all of its locks vanish. An engram may exist unactivated as a floater for any number of years or for the entire duration of an individual's life. At any future moment after the receipt of an engram, whether that time period consists of days or decades, the floater may reactivate at which time it becomes part of the command obeyed by the analytical mind in its efforts to rationalize. The removal of the individual from his restimulators, which is to say, the environment in which the engram was reactive, is in itself a form of therapy, since the engram may then return to its status as a floater.

29

Example: *Engram*—At birth occurs the phrase, "no good," uttered during a moment of headache and gasping on the part of a child.

Lock: At the age of seven while the child was ill with a minor malady, the mother in a fit of rage said that he was "no good."

The removal of the engram also removes, ordinarily without further attention, the lock.

Note: Birth remained inactive in the above case as a floater until the moment of reduced analytical power at the age of seven when a birth phrase was repeated. It is worth remarking that the entire content of the birth engram is given simultaneously both to the child and to the mother, with only the difference of somatics. It is further worthy of note that the mother quite often perceives in the child a restimulator and uses against it the phrases which were said when the child gave the mother the greatest pain, namely, birth. The child is then victimized into various psychosomatic ills by the repetition of its birth engram restimulators, which may develop even more seriously into actual disease.

---

26.   exhaust: 6. to draw out or drain off completely.

The brain controls the multiple and complex functions of the growth and condition of the organism. Containing organic sensation as one of its perceptics, the engram then, when reactivated, causes a somatic and additionally may deny body fluids, i.e., hormones[27] and blood, to some portion of the anatomy,[28] occasioning psychosomatic ills. The denial of fluid or adequate blood supply may result in a potentially infective area. The psychosomatic reduces the resistance of some portion of the body to actual disease.

Somatic and other sensory errors find their basis in unconscious antagonistic moments. A somatic may be adjusted by an address to a lock but the permanency of adjustment obtains[29] only until such time as the engram is again reactivated, causing another lock.

All aberrations are occasioned by engrams.

An engram is severely painful or severely threatening to the survival of the organism and is an engram only if it cannot be reached by the awake analytical mind.

A simple approximation of the action of an engram can be accomplished by an experiment in hypnotism whereby a positive suggestion[30] which contains a posthypnotic[31] signal is delivered to an amnesia-[32]tranced person. The subject, having been commanded to forget the suggestion when awake, will then perform the act. This suggestion is then actually a light portion of the reactive mind. It is literally interpreted, unquestionably followed, since it is received during a period of unawareness of the analytical mind or some portion of it. The restimulator, which may be the act of the operator adjusting his tie, causes the subject to commit some act. The subject will then try to explain why he is doing what he is doing, no matter how illogical that action may be. The posthypnotic suggestion is then recalled to the subject's mind and he remembers it. The compulsion vanishes (unless it is laid upon an actual engram).

27. hormone: 1. a substance formed in some organ of the body . . . [glands] and carried by a body fluid to another organ or tissue, where it has a specific effect.
28. anatomy: 2. the structure of an animal or plant or any of its parts.
29. obtain: 1. to be in force or in effect; prevail.
30. positive suggestion: suggestion by the operator to a hypnotized subject with the sole end of creating a changed mental condition in the subject by implantation of the suggestion alone. It is the transplantation of something in the hypnotist's mind into the patient's mind. The patient is then to believe it and take it as part of himself.
31. posthypnotic: of, having to do with or carried out in the period following a hypnotic trance.
32. amnesia: partial or total loss of memory caused by brain injury or by shock, repression, etc.

The obedience of the subject to the command has, as its source, engramic thought. The explanation by the subject for his own action is the analytical mind observing the organism, which it supposes is in its sole charge, and justifying itself. The release of the posthypnotic suggestion into the analytical mind brings about rational thought.

Engrams can be considered to be painfully inflicted, often timeless, posthypnotic suggestions delivered antagonistically to the "unconscious" subject. The posthypnotic suggestion given the subject in the above example would not have any permanent effect on the subject even if it were not removed by the operator, because there was presumed to be no antagonism involved (unless, of course, it rested on a former engram).

31

The physio-animal mind of an organism never ceases recording on some level. The exact moment when recording begins in an organism has not at this date been accurately determined. It has been found to be very early, probably earlier than four months after conception[33] and five months before birth. In the presence of pain, any moment prior to the age of two years may be considered to be unanalytical. Any painful experience received by the fetus[34] contains its full perceptic package, including darkness.

Once an auditor has worked a prenatal[35] engram and has seen its influence upon the engramic chain and the awake life of the adult, no question will remain in his mind concerning the actuality of the experience. That the fetus does record is attributable to a phenomenon of the extension of perceptions during moments of pain and the absence of the analytical mind.

Laboratory experiment demonstrates that under hypnosis an individual's sensory perception may be artificially extended.

The existence of pain in any large degree is sufficient to extend the hearing of the fetus so that it records, during the existence of pain and the presence of exterior sound, the entire and complete

---

33. conception: 1. a conceiving (1. to become pregnant with; cause to begin life in the womb) or being conceived in the womb.
34. fetus: 2. in man, the offspring in the womb from the end of the third month of pregnancy until birth.
35. prenatal: existing or taking place before birth.

record of the experience. As a chronic engram is but precariously[36] fixed on the mind, the syllables or voice timbres contained in the prenatal will reactivate the somatic and the emotional engramic content whenever the approximations of that engram appear in the child's (or the adult's) vicinity.

The understanding of language is not necessary to reactivate an engram since the recording of the brain is so precise that the utterance of the identical words in similar tones during later prenatal periods or during birth, or immediately after birth, can and may occasion the original prenatal or any of the prenatals to become reactive, producing locks, injuring the health of the infant or, for that matter, of the fetus.

The perceptics of the fetus are extended only during moments of pain. But a chain of prenatal engrams can occasion a condition wherein the hearing of the fetus is chronically extended, forming numerous locks before birth. These locks will vanish when the actual engrams are discovered and exhausted from the psyche.[37]

Any painful unanalytical moment containing antagonism is not only a matter of record but a source of potential action in the human organism at any period during its lifetime, reserving, of course, the question of when the fetus first begins to record.

Birth is ordinarily a severely painful unconscious experience. It is ordinarily an engram of some magnitude. Anyone who has been born then possesses at least one engram. Any period of absence of analytical power during receipt of physical pain has some engramic potentiality.

Moments when the analytical power is present in some quantity, when physical pain is absent and only antagonism to the organism is present do not form engrams and are *not* responsible for the aberration of the individual.

32

36.　precarious: 4a. dependent on chance circumstances, unknown conditions or uncertain developments; uncertain.
37.　psyche: 1. the human soul.

Sociological maladjustments;[38] parental punishments of a minor sort, even when they include pain; libidos;[39] childhood struggles and jealousies are not capable of aberrating the individual. These can influence the personality and environmental adjustment of the individual but so long as he is not pathologically[40] incompetent, he can and will resolve these problems and remain without aberration.

The human mind is an enormously powerful organism and its analytical ability is great. It is not overlaid above naturally unsocial or evil desires, but is founded upon powerful and constructive basics which only powerful, painful and antagonistic experiences can impede. Engrams will be found to have been conceived by the individual as intensely antagonistic to the survival of the organism.

33

The discovery of the basic[41] engram is the first problem of the auditor. It normally results in an engramic chain. The content of that chain will be found to be physically severe.

An engram is physically painful, is conceived by the organism as an antagonistic threat to its survival, and is received during the absence of the analytical power of the mind. These factors may vary within the engram so that an engram may be of minimal pain, maximal antagonism and minimal absence of the analytical power.

Note: One has as much functioning analyzer as one has awareness of now.

The body is to some degree reliving the experience of the engram whenever the experience is restimulated. A chronic psychosomatic, such as a painful arm, indicates the chronic, continuous coexistence with *now* of the moment the arm was broken or hurt. Several engrams reactivated into a chronic state bring several moments of unconsciousness, pain and antagonism into a coexistence

---

38. maladjustment: c. lack of harmony between the individual and his environment.
39. libido: 1. the sexual urge or instinct.
40. pathological: 2. due to or involving disease.
41. basic: the first experience recorded in mental image pictures of that type of pain, sensation, discomfort, etc. Every chain has its basic. It is a peculiarity and a fact that when one gets down to the basic on a chain, (a) it erases and (b) the whole chain vanishes for good. Basic is simply earliest.

with *now*. The engram is a bundle of perceptics which include, as the primary manifestation, organic sensation. The organic sensation is enforced on the members of the body to a greater or lesser degree whenever, and as long as, the engram is restimulated. There is only *one* psychosomatic command which is common to all engrams. Any engram contains this as part of the command it will enforce upon the body. As a stomach may be made to ache chronically (ulcers), to feel broken, the engram also enforces a command upon the *organ* of the analytical mind. That command is common to every engram. Engrams are valid only when they are received during a momentary dispersal or shocked, null condition of the analytical mind.

34

Every engram contains and enforces the command on the analytical mind that *it has been dispersed and is not operating*. This is common to every engram. This is reduction of the intellect by engrams totally aside from specific engramic content. It explains at once insanity and also the remarkable mental facility of a cleared or released[42] individual. □

---

42.   Release: an individual from whom mental stress and anxiety have been removed by Dianetics therapy.

CHAPTER SIX

Aberrations

$\mathbf{A}$ll aberrations of any kind are of precisely the same 35
nature (as covered in the last chapter). It is the content of the engram
which causes the aberration and forms its nature. Complexity
amongst engramic contents may demonstrate a most complex aberration.

The various commands contained in the engrams, reac-
tivating and modifying the basic dynamic command of the mind,
produce abnormal characteristics in the behavior of the analytical
mind, which are chronic[1] or sporadic[2] as the engrams occasioning
them are restimulated. An entire concept of existence may be built
from engramic content. Conflicts in the commands contained in
engrams and conflicts between the basic drive and the engramic
contents combine into behavior patterns.

When the organism has become so impeded that it can no
longer influence or command its environment, it can be considered
to be insane in that environment. Change of environment may
relieve the condition or, more certainly, the exhaustion of the content
of the reactive mind will restore the ability of the analytical mind to
solve the problems with which it is confronted.

Whatever the engramic content of the reactive mind and
its potential influence upon the behavior of the individual, it does
not necessarily follow that the reactive mind may be chronically
restimulated. However, when the reactive mind has been restimulated consistently, the analytical mind, called upon to solve the
problems around and through antagonistic and incorrect data, may

---

1.   chronic: 1. affecting a person for a long time.
2.   sporadic: 1. happening from time to time; not constant or regular; occasional.

be unable to perform its task. In the absence of disease or injury, any mind not in a physiological amnesia state may be restored to normal function by the removal of the reactive mind. It should be noted however that this is modified by the fact that people who have received insulin shocks,[3] prefrontal lobotomies,[4] electric shocks and other treatments are regarded as equivocal[5] and are temporarily classed with disease cases for lack of adequate observation in this stage of the experimental research.

36

People can be regarded as rational or irrational only insofar as they react in their customary environment. But any person in possession of a reactive mind is an unknown quantity until that reactive mind has been examined.

There are several factors contained in the engrams in the reactive mind which most certainly tend toward aberration. These include engramic commands which derange the time sense of the individual and thus apparently destroy his time track, and engrams which contain restimulators of such timelessness and such perceptic content that they remain thereafter continually with the individual and seem to arrest him or regress him in time. Engrams containing commands which make the individual chronically unable to conceive differences are especially harmful since these tend to compare everything to engramic value and thus cause the individual to arrive at a chronic state of engramic thinking.

The mind resolves problems related to survival, utilizing its ability to conceive similarities and observe differences.

Engrams which destroy or tend to hold in suspension the analytical mind's ability to conceive associations most influence the apparent intelligence of the mind. But engrams which tend, by their command content, to destroy the mind's ability to conceive differences may produce severe aberration.

Example: "All men are alike," received as powerful engramic content would tend to compare and associate every man

---

3.   insulin shock: a state of collapse caused by a decrease in blood sugar resulting from the administration of excessive insulin.

4.   prefrontal lobotomy: uses a scalpel or ice pick to perform an operation on the prefrontal lobes of the brain.

5.   equivocal: 2. uncertain; undecided; doubtful.

with those men contained in the reactive mind as painful and dangerous.

An aberration may attain any form or complexion.[6] As a rough analogy: A compulsion may be conceived to be an engramic command that the organism *must* do something; a repression is a command that the organism must *not* do something; a neurosis is an emotional state containing conflicts and emotional data inhibiting the abilities or welfare of the individual; and a psychosis is a conflict of commands which seriously reduce the individual's ability to solve his problems in his environment to a point where he cannot adjust some vital phase of his environmental needs.

37

All this variety of manifestation of aberration is occasioned by the pain-enforced commands or contents of engrams.

Physical aberrations are occasioned by engrams when they are not the result of injury or disease; even then, the aspect may be improved by the exhaustion of the reactive mind of the sick individual. The engram cannot manifest itself as a mental aberration without also manifesting itself to some degree as somatic aberration. Removal of the somatic content of engrams, which is also necessary to obtain any other relief, may occasion glandular readjustment, cellular inhibition and other physiological corrections.   □

---

6.   complexion: 3. general appearance or nature; character; aspect.

CHAPTER SEVEN

The Tone Scale

The tone scale denotes numerically, first the status of an engram in the reactive mind, next its erasure[1] or reduction, and provides a measure for sanity in an individual.

The derivation of this scale is clinical and is based upon observation of engrams being worked. When an engram is located and developed,[2] the extreme range it can follow begins with apathy, develops into anger (or the various facets of antagonism), proceeds into boredom and arrives at last in cheerfulness or vanishes utterly.

The tone scale is essentially an assignation of numerical value by which individuals can be numerically classified. It is not arbitrary but will be found to approximate some actual governing law in nature.

Zero is equivalent to death. An individual with a zero tone would be dead.

Ranging upwards from 0 to 1 is then that emotional bracket which may be denoted as apathy along its graduated scale from death to the beginnings of apathetic resentment.

From 1 to 2 is the range of antagonism, including suspicion, resentment and anger.

Boredom and its equivalents, by which is denoted minor annoyance, begin at 2 and end at 3.

39

1.　erasure: when applied to an engram which has been treated means that the engram has disappeared from the engram bank; it cannot be found afterwards except by search of the standard memory.
2.　develop: 3. to become known or apparent; be disclosed.

From 3 to 4 are the emotions which range from care-lessness to cheerfulness.

The term *tone four* denotes a person who has achieved rationality and cheerfulness.

40
Each engram residual in the reactive mind has its own independent tonal value. Serious engrams will be found in the apathy range. Dangerous engrams will be found in the anger range. Above 2.5 an engram could not be considered to have any great power to affect the analytical mind. Each engram in the reactive mind then can be said to possess a tone value. The composite sum of these engrams will give, if added, a numerical value to the reactive mind.

Engrams can be computed as they lie along the dynamics, and to each dynamic may be assigned a tone. The sum of the tones of the dynamics, divided by the number of the dynamics will give a potential numerical value for an individual. This, of course, is variable depending on the existence of restimulators in his environment to reactivate the engrams.

The probable average of mankind at this writing may be in the vicinity of 3.0. Complete rationality depends upon exhaustion of the reactive mind and complete rationality is invariably the result of reaching tone 4.

The initial diagnosis is done by the assignation of a general tone to denote the condition of an individual's reactive mind.

His methods of meeting life, his emotional reaction to the problems in his environment, can be evaluated by the use of the tone scale.

In auditing, as will be covered later, an engram normally can be expected to run from its initial value in the apathy or anger range to tone 4. Very shortly after it reaches tone 4 it should vanish. If it vanishes without attaining the laughter of tone 4 it can be assumed that the individual's basic engram has not been erased.

The tone scale has value in auditing and should be thoroughly understood. □

CHAPTER EIGHT

The Character of Engrams

There are several general types of engrams. It must be understood that the mind possesses a time track of one sort or another and that this track is a specific thing. The time track of an individual will include all those things available to his analytical mind when in a light trance or during regression.[1] However, a person can be regressed and the data which he can easily contact along his time track is definitely not engramic even if it possesses an emotional charge. Everything on this track will be rational or justified experience. It will not include engrams. It may include locks—which is to say that it may include moments of mental anguish or antagonism and may even include instants of unconsciousness which have some slight engramic command value.

41

An engram has several specific, positive characteristics. It is received by the individual at some moment of physical pain. It is not available to the analyzer and it includes conceived or actual antagonism to the survival of the organism. Certain mechanics such as "forget it" may swerve a minimumly painful or unconscious experience off the time track. In that case it becomes possessed of engramic command value.

All engrams with power to derange the analytical mind and aberrate the physical body lie off the time track and are not available to the analytical mind.

By reason of its disorganization during the moment the engram was received, or because it has been forcibly instructed that the data in the engram is not to be recalled, the analyzer cannot reach

---

1. regression: was a technique by which part of the individual's self remained in the present and part went back to the past. These abilities of the mind were supposed native only in hypnotism and were used only in hypnotic techniques.

the engram by ordinary means because the data has been erroneously labeled "dangerous," "important" or "too painful to touch." The engram then, by a bypass circuit, feeds hidden commands into the analyzer. By a direct instantaneous circuit it is permanently connected to the motor controls, all perceptic channels, the glands and heart. It is awaiting a moment of low general tone, weariness or injury when the analytical mind has reduced powers. It is also awaiting the perception of one or more of the engram's restimulators in the environment of the organism.

42   Continuous restimulation of the engrams can, in itself, cause a low general tone which in its turn permits more engrams to become restimulated. As the reactive mind comes into a more or less completely chronic state of restimulation, the individual becomes more and more governed by this mind. His thought becomes more and more engramic and he can be seen to drop in general tone on the tone scale down to the break point which may be arbitrarily placed somewhere between 2 and 2.5 and below which lies the region of insanity.

Engramic thought is irrational, identity thought by which the mind is made to conceive identities where only vague similarities may exist. It is necessary that the auditor thoroughly understand engramic thought, for it is with this complete irrationality of identity that he will basically deal. As he works with any preclear he must continually employ in the bulk of his computation on the case the equation of engramic thinking.

Engramic thinking can be stated by: A equals A equals A equals A equals A.

The engram, when one or more of its restimulators is perceived in the environment during a moment of low general tone, may dramatize. The dramatization *is* the precise content of the engram. The aberration is the precise content of the engram. The reaction of an individual's analytical mind when an engram is reactivated is justification.

There is reason to believe that part of this survival mechanism consists of the axiom: **The analyzer must never permit an incorrect solution.** The engram brings about many incorrect solutions. The analyzer may very well become entirely involved with the attempt to discover and deliver to a society, or to itself, adequate rational reasons for the behavior of the organism.

The analytical mind, though working from the command of the engram itself, is unaware of the source of the command. Not being able to discover the source, it introverts more and more in an effort to solve a problem which contains danger to the organism. The analytical mind tends to find the danger without and within the organism.

43

There are five ways that the organism can react to a danger in its vicinity. It can attack it, avoid it, neglect it, run from it or succumb[2] to it. In just these ways can the analytical mind, which, it must be remembered, *is* possessed of self-determinism and willpower, react to the reactive mind. As the general tone lowers, as the analytical mind becomes less and less powerful through weariness, continual reverses[3] in general health, etc., the more and more heed it must give to the problems unsolved in the reactive mind. These are in essence unsolved problems. As such, they contain their own solutions. The analytical mind, unable to reach them, justifies the organism's reaction to them (succumbs to them), causes the organism to attempt to flee from them, apathetically may neglect them (as in prefrontal lobotomy), avoids them in many intricate ways or attacks them. The analytical mind is not only not certain where the experience lies on the time track, it also does not know whether the menace is within the organism or without it. So it can become entirely indiscriminate[4] and eventually it may achieve highly irrational solutions by which it seeks to solve the problems of the highly irrational reactive mind.

The deep sensory perception channel entering the mind is evidently equipped with an "appreciator" which sorts according to the momentary general tone or potential of the analytical mind. The

---

2.   succumb: 1. to give way (to); yield; submit.
3.   reverse: 4. a change from good fortune to bad; defeat.
4.   indiscriminate: 2. not discriminating (to recognize the difference between); not making careful choices or distinctions.

higher the general tone or potential of the analytical mind the better the data in the appreciator is sorted. The appreciator circuits are evidently fully apprised of engramic content in the reactive mind and evaluate restimulators perceived in the environment against the general tone of the analytical mind. When that is low, restimulators route more or less directly to the reactive mind which instantly responds by fixed connections into the motor controls. Commands to the various members, muscles, glands and organs of the body may be sporadic or constant, producing a high variety of responses in the body. Entire vocabularies are fed into the voice circuits directly from the reactive mind when an engram is restimulated. Orders to be active or inactive are fed to other portions. The individual time track of the engram spaces the commands to the organism and a dramatization is accomplished which may contain a portion or all of the content of the engram as governed by the situation. Psychosomatic ills, hysterias,[5] rages, tantrums,[6] criminal acts and any and all content prejudicial to the survival of the organism in which the organism is seen to be indulging has as its source the reactive mind.

The sole and only content of the reactive mind is *what exterior sources have done to the organism.*

None of the content of the reactive mind is self-motivated. The auditor is then interested only in what is done *to* the person, not what the person himself has done, since, for purposes of auditing, the acts of the organism in its society can be discounted[7] beyond diagnosis. Even then they are of small importance to the auditor.

An organism possessed of an analytical mind, not victimized by incapacitating disease or injury (and unimpeded) will commit no act knowingly prejudicial[8] to the survival of the organism or other facets within the dynamics. It will combat only those dangers in society which are actual menaces.

---

5. hysteria: 2. any outbreak of wild, uncontrolled excitement or feeling, such as fits of laughing and crying.
6. tantrum: a violent, willful outburst of annoyance, rage, etc.; childish fit of bad temper.
7. discount: 1. to disregard partly or wholly.
8. prejudicial: 1. tending to injure or impair.

Whatever may be the status of the "innate[9] moral sense," the basic intent of the basic personality is to further various energy forms along the dynamics toward the goal. Only moments of actual dispersal of the awareness of the analytical mind permit data to be received which is prejudicial to the intent of the dynamics. Only from these "unconscious" moments can the basically stable and enormously powerful and able analytical mind be aberrated through the implantation of unanalyzed, painfully administered and antagonistic information. It is the purpose of the auditor to find and exhaust these moments from the life of the individual. Dianetic auditing includes therefore, as its basic principle, the exhaustion of all the painfully unconscious moments of a subject's life. By eradicating pain from the life of an individual, the auditor returns the individual to complete rationality and sanity.

45

The auditor should never be content with merely bringing the person back to normal. He should achieve with the person a tone four even though this is far in advance of the average state of society at this time. A tone four with his drives intact and powerful, with his rationality and intelligence increased to the optimum, becomes extremely valuable to the society, whatever his past.

Knowing this the auditor can expect a maximum result of lasting duration with any preclear not physically hopeless.

The entire purpose of the auditor is to rehabilitate the basic dynamic and the normal purpose or profession of the individual whom he audits. Anything implanted by positive suggestion or "education" in the course of auditing is harmful and must be canceled if delivered. Only the basic personality of the individual can decide and evaluate things in his environment. Therefore, hypnotism as practiced with positive suggestions should be shunned since any and all hypnotic commands with the attendant forgetter[10] mechanisms are no more than artificially implanted engrams. Indeed, it is quite usual for the auditor to have to exhaust hypnotically implanted material received either from some hypnotist or from the analytical mind itself when the person has been operating under auto-control.[11]

---

9.   innate: 1a. existing naturally rather than acquired; that seems to have been in one from birth.

10.   forgetter: any engram command which makes the individual believe he can't remember.

11.   auto-control: autohypnosis used in Dianetics is probably as close to fruitless masochism as one can get. If a patient places himself in autohypnosis and regresses himself in an effort to reach illness or birth or prenatals, the only thing he will get is ill.

Hypnotism as such does not work, and a study and short practice in Dianetics will reveal exactly why.

The auditor is attempting to delete the reactive mind from the individual. This reactive mind is an infestation of foreign, careless and unreasoning commands which disrupt the self-determinism of the individual to such an extent that he no longer has charge, through his analytical mind, of the organism itself, but finds himself under the continual and chronic orders of unseen, never-reviewed exterior forces, often and usually antipathetic to the survival of the organism.

46

Engrams deal with identities where no identities exist. They therefore pose many strange and irrational problems which are seen as aberrations in preclears. If a human being has been born, he can be supposed to have at least one engram. Anyone who has a birth which has not been cleared by therapy has therefore a reactive mind. There is no disgrace attached to having a reactive mind since it was thrust without his consent and without his knowledge upon an unconscious and helpless individual. Sometimes this was done by persons with the best of imaginable intentions. A person not possessed of a rational mind cannot be rationally considered to be morally responsible, no matter the demands of the current society which hitherto lacked any method of determining responsibility.

The pain contained in the reactive mind is normally severe. The usual parental punishments, family complications, reprimands, minor accidents and the battle of the individual with his environment, influence but do not cause a reactive mind, nor do these things have the power to change materially the reactions of an individual.

In the background of any individual exist many hidden personalities contained in the reactive mind. Dealing in identities, the reactive mind often confuses identities of individuals. Therefore, irrational attachments and antipathies are formed by aberrated individuals who can often find no reason for such attachments or antipathies in their contemporary[12] environment.

---

12.   contemporary: 2. up-to-date.

The content of an engram is literally interpreted, not as it was stated to the "unconscious" subject, but as it was received in its most literal phraseology[13] and perception.

The organism possesses many inherent[14] mechanisms and abilities by which it can learn or preserve or forward itself along the dynamics. Any one of them may be exaggerated by engrams to a point where it becomes an actual threat to the organism or impedes it. Engrams can and do aberrate all the sensory perceptions, any and all parts of the body and the mind itself. By demanding suicide the engram can destroy the entire organism.

47

The error of the reactive mind was introduced by the evolution of speech, for which the basic mechanism was not designed. When all perceptics save speech formed the reactive mind, it was to some degree serviceable. With speech came such complexities of perception and such interchanges of ideas that a whole series of illusions[15] and delusions[16] could be derived from the reactive mind's necessity to determine identities for purposes of emergency.

With speech the reactive mind came to possess far more power and extensive content. The analytical mind, being a delicate mechanism in some respects no matter how rugged and capable in others, then could become subjected to delusions and illusions which, however shadowy and unreal, must nevertheless be obeyed. By stripping the reactive mind of its past painful content the analytical mind may be placed in complete command of the organism.

The moment a man or a group becomes possessed of this ability, it becomes possessed of self-determinism. So long as these possess reactive minds, irrationalities will persist. Because it contains literal speech, no reactive mind can be conceived to be of any value whatsoever to the rational organism since the methods of that reactive mind remain intact and will continue to act to preserve the organism in times of "unconsciousness" of the analytical mind. There is no residual good in any reactive mind. It is capable of any illusion. It has no assist power along the dynamics save only to cancel or

---

13.   phraseology: choice and pattern of words; way of speaking or writing.
14.   inherent: existing in something as a natural or permanent characteristic or quality.
15.   illusion: suggests the false perception or interpretation of something that has objective existence.
16.   delusion: implies belief in something that is contrary to fact or reality, resulting from deception, a misconception or a mental disorder.

modify other reactive mind content. The source of the individual's power and purpose is not derived from the reactive mind but from the basic dynamic and its eight divisions. Any auditor will establish this to his own satisfaction after he has run a very few cases.

When an individual during auditing is attempting to "hold on to his aberrations," the auditor may be assured that that person has as part of the content of the reactive mind such phrases as, "don't dare get rid of it," which, identically translated, apparently applies to aberrations. It may, in fact, apply in an engram containing an attempted abortion.

The identity factor in the reactive mind may cause the analytical mind to respond irrationally in auditing and to justify the aberrations in many irrational ways. Whatever means he uses or statements he makes to avoid the exhaustion of his reactive mind is contained exactly in the reactive mind as a positive suggestion and has no application whatsoever in rational thought.

Individuality (if by that is meant a man's desires and habits) is not traced to the reactive mind save when by individuality is meant those flagrant[17] eccentricities[18] which pass in Dickens[19] for characters.

A man is much more an individual after his reactive mind has been cleared. □

---

17. flagrant: very bad and obvious.
18. eccentricity: 2. deviation from what is ordinary or customary, as in conduct or manner; oddity; unconventionality.
19. Dickens, Charles: English novelist of the late 19th century noted for picturesque and extravagant characters in the lower economic strata of England at that time.

CHAPTER NINE

Dramatization

Dramatization is the duplication of an engramic content, entire or in part, by an aberree in his present-time environment. Aberrated conduct is entirely dramatization. Aberrated conduct will occur only when and if an engram exists in the reactive mind of the aberree. That conduct will be a duplication of such an engram. The degree of dramatization is in direct ratio to the degree of restimulation of the engrams causing it. A mild dramatization would be a similarity to the engram. A severe dramatization would be an identity with the engram.

49

The general tone of an aberree, when high—when his person is unwearied and he is well and not directly menaced in his environment—does not permit as great an influence by the reactive mind, since the tone level of the entire individual possesses too great a differential[1] from the tone of the engram. As the general tone of the individual approaches the tone level of the engram under restimulation, dramatization becomes more severe.

The analytical mind is present to the degree that the general tone of the aberree is high. As this general tone lowers through ill health, reverses or constant restimulation of the reactive mind, the analytical mind is proportionately less aware. Dramatization is demonstrated by the aberree in inverse ratio to the potential of the analytical mind. A geometrical progression[2] is entered as general tone lowers to cause the analytical mind to lose its entire awareness potential. Since every engram contains, as the common denominator of all engrams, the unconsciousness of the organ which

---

1.   differential: 6. a difference between comparable things.
2.   geometrical progression: progression with a constant ratio between successive quantities, as
        1:3:9:27:81.

is the analytical mind, dramatizations gain rapidly as this inter-action progresses.

In the presence of a relatively high analytical mind aware-ness potential, dramatization takes the form of similarity. The data of the engram is present but is interspersed[3] with or modified by justified thought. The physical pain which is always present as part of the dramatization is equally mild, a duplication of the pain which was present during the engram. The awareness potential of the analytical mind reduces in the restimulation of the engram which again reduces the general tone.

50

The aberree is subject to almost continuous dramatization of one engram or another as the restimulators appear in his vicinity. (Although the aberration may be so mild as to include only some chronically affected organ.) Complete dramatization is complete iden-tity. It is the engram in full force in present time with the aberree taking one or more parts of the dramatis personae[4] present in the engram. He may dramatize all the actors or merely one of them. His dramatization is identity, is unreasoned and always entirely reac-tive. When the analytical mind reaches the low point of awareness potential it held during the engramic incident, that point is also forced upon the aberree as a part of the dramatization. The aberree may also dramatize himself as he was at the moment of the engram's receipt.

The words, physical actions, expressions and emotions of an aberree undergoing an identity dramatization are those of the single or various dramatis personae present in the engram.

An engram which can be dramatized may at any time in an aberree's future be dramatized as an identity dramatization, when and if his general tone is low and his environment becomes infil-trated by restimulators.

An aberree, because of high general tone and other factors, may not suffer the restimulation of an engram for a number of years after its receipt. A large number of engrams may be present and

---

3.   intersperse: 1. to scatter among other things; put here and there or at intervals.
4.   dramatis personae: 1. the characters in a play or story [used here to refer to people present in the engrams of the aberree].

undramatized in any aberree, if he has never been presented with their particular restimulators in an optimum moment for restimulation. The common denominator of all insanity is the absence of all or almost all awareness potential in the analytical mind. Insanity can be acute[5] or chronic. Any identity dramatization is insanity, by which is meant the entire absence of rationality.

The aberree commonly and chronically dramatizes locks. The engramic content may compel or repress the aberree whenever restimulated.

51

An irrational person is irrational to the degree that he dramatizes or succumbs to engramic content in his reactive mind. The computations which can be made on the basis of dramatization are infinite. The reactive mind thinks in identities. Dramatizations are severe as they approach identity with the engrams which force them into being in the conduct of the aberree.

The dianeticist can profit in many ways by these principles of dramatization. By examination of the rage or apathy or hysteria patterns of the preclear, the dianeticist will find himself in possession of the exact character of the engrams for which he is searching.

In the case of the manic,[6] the fanatic or the zealot, an engram has entirely blocked at least one of the purpose lines deriving from a dynamic. The engram may be called an "assist engram." Its own surcharge (not the dynamic force) leads the individual to believe that he has a high purpose which will permit him to escape pain. This "purpose" is a false purpose not ordinarily sympathetic[7] with the organism, having a hectic quality derived from the pain which is part of it, even though that pain is not wittingly experienced. This "assist engram" is using the native ability of the organism to accomplish its false "purpose" and brings about a furious and destructive effort on the part of the individual who, without this "assist engram" could have better accomplished the same goal. The worst feature of the "assist engram" is that the effort it commands is engramic dramatization of a particular sort, and if the engram itself is restimulated the individual becomes subject to the physical pain and

---

5.   acute: 4. brief and severe.
6.   manic: a person exhibiting excessive or unreasonable enthusiasm.
7.   sympathetic: 3. showing favor, approval or agreement.

fear which the entire experience contained. Therefore, the false purpose itself is subject to sporadic *sag*.[8] This sag becomes longer and longer in duration between periods of false thrust. It is easy to confuse, in casual observation, an "assist engram" and an actual, valid drive, unless one also observes the interspersed periods of sag. The "assist engram" may or may not occasionally accomplish something, but it does accomplish a confusion in the society that the dynamics of the individual are derived from his bad experiences. This is a thing which is emphatically[9] untrue.

52   Inherently the individual has great willpower. This however can be aberrated. Willpower or its absence occasions the attitude of the aberree toward his reactive mind.

The prevention of the dramatization of an engram or a lock further reduces dynamic thrust of the aberree. Chronic prevention lowers his general tone toward the break point. Unhampered dramatization, as it contains restimulation of a physical pain and the reduced potential of the analytical mind, produces other harmful effects.

Necessity can and does render inactive the entire reactive mind.

Dramatization occurs most often in the absense of necessity or when the reactive mind has obscured the presence of necessity.

Dramatization is residual in the motor controls including speech and can be allayed[10] by the physical exhaustion of the individual. The organism during dramatization tends to revivify[11] toward the moment of the engram's occurrence—the engram containing, as one of its identity parts, the complete physical condition of the organism as at the moment of laying in of the engram.

There is no folly or facet of human activity which cannot be dramatized. An immediate alleviation can be achieved when

8.   sag: 3. to lose firmness, strength or intensity; weaken through weariness, age, etc.; droop.
9.   emphatic: 1. . . . decidedly; decisively.
10.   allay: 2. to lessen, relieve or alleviate.
11.   revivify: relive.

addressing an aberree who is in identity dramatization by acting upon the fact that the conditions of auditing, with no exception, already exist; i.e., the preclear returned to the moment of occurrence. Affinity may be established and Dianetic auditing begun at once. He can be persuaded to listen for the phrases he is uttering and they can be alleviated by exhaustion on routine procedure. □

CHAPTER TEN

The Auditor's Code

Not because it is a pleasant thing to do or because it is a noble[1] idea, the auditor must always treat a preclear in a certain definite way which can be outlined as the Auditor's Code. Failure to follow this code will cause trouble to the auditor, will considerably lengthen and disturb his work and may endanger the preclear.

55

The auditor in the first place, at the optimum, should be himself cleared; otherwise he will find that many of his own engrams are restimulated as he listens to the engrams of his preclears. This restimulation may cause his own engrams to become chronic, victimizing him with various allergies[2] and delusions and causing him to be, at best, extremely uncomfortable.

An auditor can audit while he himself is being cleared as this is a peculiar and special method of locating his own engrams, since they become restimulated. Becoming painful to him, they can be found and speedily removed.

Even if he is not himself cleared, the auditor must act like a Clear toward the preclear. The Auditor's Code is the natural activity of a Clear.

The auditor must act toward the preclear exactly in the way that the preclear as an organism would desire that his own conscious analytical mind would react to and consider the organism.

An affinity must therefore be maintained at all costs. The auditor must never permit himself to lose his temper, become

1.   noble: 3b. very good or excellent; superior of its kind.
2.   allergy: a condition producing an unfavorable reaction to certain foods, pollens, etc.

aggravated, to scold or badger or antagonize the preclear in any way. To do so would not merely disturb the comfort of the preclear but might additionally derange him and might even prohibit further beneficial therapy by the auditor.

The code is nearly "Christlike."

The auditor must be confident in that he must continually reassure the preclear when restimulated engrams cause despondency[3] on the preclear's part. A cheerful optimistic presence encourages the preclear through his most painful experiences.

The auditor must be courageous, never permitting himself to be intimidated[4] by either the aggression or hostility of the preclear.

The auditor must be kind, never indulging in hostilities or personal prejudices. The auditor must be trustworthy, never betraying or capriciously[5] denying a preclear and above all never breaking his word to the preclear. An auditor must be clean for personal odors or bad breath may be restimulators to the preclear or may disturb him. The auditor must take care not to offend the concepts or sensibilities of the preclear.

The auditor must be persistent, never permitting the case of the preclear to either resist him or to remain unsolved until it is in a proper tone 4, since the restimulation of engrams is a malady unto itself unless they are being properly exhausted.

The auditor must be patient, never hurrying or harassing the preclear beyond the needs of stirring an engram into view. He must be willing to work at any and all times necessary and for the length of time necessary to exhaust the engrams in process of elimination.

In addition to these things it may be remarked that a definite affinity is established between the auditor and preclear during the auditing. In the case of opposite sexes this affinity may

56

---

3.   despondency: loss of courage or hope; dejection.
4.   intimidate: 1. to make timid; make afraid.
5.   capricious: characterized by or subject to whim; impulsive and unpredictable.

amount to an infatuation.[6] The auditor must remain aware of this and know that he can and should redirect the infatuation to some person or activity other than himself when auditing is at an end. Not to do so is to produce an eventual situation wherein the preclear may have to be rebuffed[7] with consequent trouble for the auditor.   □

---

6.   infatuate: 2. to inspire with foolish or shallow love or affection.
7.   rebuff: 1. a blunt or abrupt rejection, as of a person's advances.

CHAPTER ELEVEN

Auditing

The auditing technique consists of assisting the preclear's analytical mind or some part of it with the auditor's analytical mind. The auditor then functions during each successive period of auditing, and only during the periods themselves, as an extra analytical mind of the preclear.

The reactive mind was received during the dispersal or inactivity of the analytical mind. The reactive mind is removed by "returning"[1] the preclear to the engram, and laying its contents before the scrutiny[2] of the analytical mind.

This technique may be considered the lowest common denominator of a number of techniques. *Anything* which will serve this purpose and permit auditing to be accomplished efficiently is valid technique.

The optimum is purely personal affinity brought about by understanding and communication with the preclear on agreeable subjects. Another and almost useless method is narcosynthesis[3] together with the various drugs and hypnotics used to produce sleep. Methods can be found such as faith healing, books on medical hypnosis, the techniques of Indian medicine men and so forth. It is pointless to delineate these methods here. They are currently available under the name of hypnotism but a caution should be enjoined[4] that hypnosis as itself is not at all acceptable to Dianetics

---

1. returning: the person can "send" a portion of his mind to a past period on either a mental or combined mental and physical basis and can reexperience incidents which have taken place in his past in the same fashion and with the same sensations as before.
2. scrutiny: 1. a close examination; minute inspection.
3. narcosynthesis: the practice of inducing sleep with drugs and then talking to the patient to draw out buried thoughts.
4. enjoin: 1. to urge or impose with authority; order; enforce.

and indeed has extremely limited use. Briefly, however, it must be remarked that if hypnotism is studied to advance these techniques, all positive suggestion and posthypnotic suggestion must be avoided as these suggestions depend for their effectiveness upon the already existing content of the reactive mind and will only form additional locks.

60

Any and all so-called hypnotic drugs have definite drawbacks since they, like so many other things, may be termed "shotgun" methods. These paralyze not only the analytical mind but the remainder of the organism so that it is nearly impossible to obtain the proper somatic reaction in the preclear. They are not hypnotics but anesthetics. By using them the auditor instantly denies himself the main material which will lead him to the engram, which is to say, restimulated physical pain. Such restimulated pain is never of very great magnitude and is obliterated by the use of anesthesias.

At no time should the auditor permit the preclear to be under the delusion that he is being hypnotized. This is mentioned because hypnotism is a current fad and the principles of Dianetics have nothing whatever to do with hypnotism. Both are based upon simple natural laws but have between them an enormous gulf. One is the tool of the charlatan[5] and the other is the science of the human mind.

Regression in its simplest form, hereafter called *return,* is employed in Dianetic auditing. It would be an extraordinary case which required revivification. Return is the method of retaining the body and the awareness of the subject in present time while he is told to go back to a certain incident. Dates are not mentioned. His size is not mentioned. Various means are used to restimulate his memory. Any of the perceptics may be employed to return him to some period of his past. He is told simply to "go back to the time when ———." He is asked to recount what he can of the incident. He is told that he is "right there" and that he can "recall this." Little else is said by the auditor save those hints necessary to return the preclear to the proper time.

---

5.   charlatan: a person who pretends to knowledge or skill; quack.

The preclear is not allowed at any moment to revivify in that period since the data is drained as a surcharge from his time track to present time. He is told that he can remember this in present time since that will occasion the somatics to return to present time. Most of the data is located by observing some somatic pain in the individual or some somatic aberration and seeking to discover wherein it was received.

The somatics are employed primarily because the motor controls possess a less disturbed time track than the sensory strip.[6] Anything which tends to lighten these somatics is then antipathetic to auditing. It must be remembered that there is no aberration without an accompanying somatic. The somatics alone, being physical ills of one sort or another, hold the aberrated content of the reactive mind in place. The motor controls can be returned to a period although the conscious or analytical mind believes itself to be entirely in present time. By talking to the muscles or motor controls or various bodily aches and pains, the auditor can shift them at will up and down their time track. This time track is not connected to the analytical mind and speech, but is apparently a parallel time track with greater reliability than the sensory track. The precision of data contained in the motor control time track is enormous. Muscles can be made to tense or relax. Coughs, aches and pains can be made to come and go simply by uttering the right words for the engrams, or the wrong words.

It is the primary task of the auditor to cause the time tracks of the motor strip and the sensory strip to come into parallel. That the time track exists in the strips has not been proven but they can so be considered for the purposes of this explanation. That they exist is extremely apparent. The motor strip time track can be asked questions down to the smallest moment of time, and the area of an engram can be so located and its character determined.

As an analogy, a dream may be considered as the reception by the remaining analytical mind of a distortedly reflected and indirectly received picture of the engrams. This applies only when the dream is specifically directed at the reactive mind. It will be found

61

---

6.   sensory strip: the sensory strip could be considered the mental side of the switchboard and the motor strip the physical side.

that a preclear with a large and active reactive mind does not dream to any great extent in normal sleep but that a Release may dream pleasantly and consistently. A dream in its normal function is that powerful and original mechanism called the imagination, compositing or creating new pictures.

The use of the dream is not highly technical and has little value in Dianetics. The auditor gleans[7] data from the preclear by his own remarks about any subject or by the preclear's illogicalness on a subject. The auditor tells the preclear to dream about this data. When the preclear has had the dream he is directed to go back to the engram causing the dream. Quite often he will do so. If he does not, or if he becomes hostile, it is certain that an engram exists on the subject.

The lie detector, the encephalograph[8] and many other means are of limited usefulness in determining both the character and the extent of the engrams since into these as into the dreams can be fed the restimulators of the preclear. A codified restimulator list can be created which will be found to be common to most preclears. It should include all types of illnesses, accidents, the common trite[9] phrases of the society and names of various persons who commonly surround a child during his childhood. Such a codified restimulator list would be interesting for experiment and every auditor can compose his own. These are best composed after auditing the individual preclear and after inquiry into his life to determine the various irrationalities of thought.

In that engrams are identity thought, the remarks of the preclear about his engrams will be found to be included in the content of those engrams. When the preclear is asked to imagine a bad situation at certain ages and under hypnotic conditions, he will very often deliver up a complete engram. The auditor must realize that every remark that a preclear makes while he is going over his reactive mind is probably some part of the content of that reactive mind. That mind is literal. The words the preclear uses when referring to it must be literally evaluated.   □

---

7.   glean: 3. to collect or gather anything little by little or slowly.
8.   encephalograph: 2. electroencephalograph (an instrument for measuring and recording the electric activity of the brain).
9.   trite: worn out by constant use; no longer having freshness, originality or novelty; stale.

CHAPTER TWELVE

Diagnosis

It is a useful and positive principle that whatever con-   63
fronts or contests the analytical mind of the preclear will also
confront and contest the analytical mind of the auditor. When the
auditor is acting as the analytical mind of the preclear, whatever
emotion or antagonism is directed toward him is the emotion or
antagonism which is directed by the reactive mind toward the
preclear's own analytical mind. If a preclear cannot hear what people
are saying in his engrams, he has another engram about "can't hear."
If he cannot feel anything in his engram, it is because he has an
engram about "can't feel." If he cannot see, he has an engram about
not being able to see, and so forth. If he cannot return, he has an
engram about going back or returning to childhood or some such
thing. If he is doubtful and skeptical about what is happening or
what has happened to him, it is because he has an engram about
being doubtful and skeptical. If he is antagonistic, his reactive mind
contains a great deal of antagonism. If he is self-conscious or em-
barrassed, it is because his reactive mind contains self-consciousness
or embarrassment. If he insists on maintaining his own control,
refusing to do what the auditor tells him to do (although he is
returned), it is because he has an engram about self-control, and so
forth and so on. This is identity thought and is used in diagnosis.

The return is the best method of learning the problems of
the preclear. Trying to work the preclear into remembrance, hearing,
seeing, feeling, going back and forward, going to sleep, awakening
and taking due notice of what he says about the entire process
will form a rather complete diagnosis on one who is not insane.
Questioning the preclear as to what is wrong with him while
returned will elicit[1] replies straight out of his principal engrams.

---

1.   elicit: to draw out (information, a response, etc.).

Listening to an endless justification of his actions is both a delay and a waste of time, but listening to what he has to say about what he thinks has happened to him or what he is afraid of is of definite value.

The insane form and pose a slightly different problem but essentially the same.

It is a clinically established observation that the reactive mind is relatively shallow. Below it lies the basic personality of the individual no matter how "insane" he may be. Therefore, by one means or another, a rational being may be reached within a person, a being which is not aberrated. It is this fact of nonaberration which makes the basic personality a difficult aid in diagnosis. Here however it can be established what the person really wants, what he hopes, what he actually feels. It has been observed that no matter what his raving[2] state, providing his brain structure is normal and complete, the basic personality is entirely sound and sane and will cooperate. After auditing, the person will become this strong, competent and able personality.

The reactive mind, when unable to exert itself to its aberrated full in the environment of the person, will break the person or cause him to lose tone. Therefore it is of definite interest to discover what immediately preceded the break of the preclear or what is currently causing him unhappiness. Something is dispersing his dynamics. The probability is that he has a chronic restimulator in his vicinity. Wives, husbands, mothers, fathers, superiors, etc., can be the source of such breaking since they turn the purpose of the reactive mind, which pretends to desire above all else the best interest of the person, back upon the person himself. Thus these sources cause the individual to lower back into the tone of the reactive mind, apathy or a low tone 2.

The problem of the fixed person and the problem of the sympathy engram[3] are both visible in the aberrated individual. The identity thought of the reactive mind has taken some part of the personality of some individual in the current environment and

64

---

2.   rave: 1. to talk wildly or furiously, to talk nonsensically in delirium; *raving mad,* completely mad.
3.   sympathy engram: an engram of a very specific nature, being the effort of the parent or guardian to be kind to a child who is severely hurt.

referred it to some part of the personality of an individual in the engramic past. The discovery of this identity is one of the principal problems in auditing. The sympathy engram is of a very specific nature, being the effort of the parent or guardian to be kind to a child who is severely hurt. If that parent or guardian has shown the child antagonism prior to the time of the injury, the adult (preclear) is prone to reactivate the injury in the presence of the identity personality with whom he is now associated. This causes many somatic ills to present themselves in the present. Only the exact words of a sympathy engram will soothe the aberrated personality.

65

There are not many personality types. A human being learns through mimicry. If his own self is found to be too painful he can become another self and very often does. A tone four can become another person at will without being aberrated about it, thus enjoying books and plays by "being" the person portrayed. But an aberrated individual can become part of the engramic cast of his reactive mind and so solve all of his problems in such an aberrated fashion. Aberrated persons are not themselves since they do not possess their own determinism.

As has been stated, those emotions, doubts, worries and problems which confront the auditor when attempting to place the preclear in reverie[4] or to work him in that reverie will lead the auditor into the basic content of the reactive mind.

There are certain definite manifestations which can be suspected and certain routines which follow every case. Every human being has been carried in the womb and every human being has been born. The discovery of the basic engram on each chain is extremely important. Finding the basic engram is like taking the enemy in the flank.[5] There is nothing before it, therefore the end most remote from the adult life of the individual is the end most exposed for the attack of the auditor.

---

4.   reverie: in reverie the preclear is placed in a light state of "concentration" which is not to be confused with hypnosis. The mind of the preclear will be found to be to some degree detachable from his surroundings and directed interiorly.

5.   flank: 3. the right or left side of a body of troops, etc.

In the basic engram the preclear can see, feel, hear and freely emote.[6] When he is returned to later incidents, it may be found that he cannot do these things no matter how hard the auditor works to enable him to do so. By pursuing the engramic chain up its chronological sequence, this ability will be restored. Therefore it is necessary first and foremost to locate the basic engram. This may, in some few cases, lie later than birth. In the majority of the cases it will be found to lie at or before birth. No discussion is here entered about the ability of the human mind to remember at such remote periods. It can be stated however that when engramic data does exist, the time track is opened by pain and antagonism at these extreme points and can be contacted and exhausted. It is with the greatest difficulty that the auditor will find the basic engram. It is ordinarily quite painful, and since the scanning mechanism has as its purpose (or one of its purposes) the avoidance of pain, it will not easily reach them. Like the scanning mechanism on a cathode ray tube,[7] the scanners of even a very reduced potential analytical mind sweep over, skipping and not touching the data on the engramic chain. By various means the auditor must then require the scanners to contact that data and force the data back onto the time track where it can be properly exhausted.

Light prenatals are the best possible approach to a case. When the only prenatal is an extremely heavy one or an attempted abortion (which, by the way, are very common), the auditor must use a great deal of guile.[8] It can be said that the basic engram and the beginning of the actual engram chains is very early, before, near or during birth, is painful, and will not be easily contacted. In that few preclears have more than a few hundred serious engrams, the task is light when once begun but requires a great deal of imagination and persuasion.

A prenatal must always be suspected unless birth, when lifted,[9] rises easily into a tone 4. If none of the engrams will rise into a tone 4, the auditor would suppose that he has not discovered the basic. There are three kinds of engrams: the precursor, the engram and the follower. By engram here is meant that experience which the auditor has found and is working upon. If it does not seem to be

---

6.   emote: to give expression to emotion.

7.   cathode ray tube: a vacuum tube, for example, a television picture tube, in which beams of electrons are directed against a fluorescent screen where they produce a luminous image.

8.   guile: slyness and cunning in dealing with others; craftiness.

9.   lift: 2. to rise and vanish; be dispelled.

lifting after a few recountings, a precursor (earlier engram) must be suspected and returned to. In this way an earlier basic may be discovered. Blows in the womb, attempted abortions and birth are the usual basics. Easily the most important are the prenatals.

When a child is abnormally afraid of the dark, he probably has a severe engramic experience in prenatal. This prenatal experience will include all the sound data and sensory data of the incident. It is idiotic and identical. The preclear will have somatics. These on the first few recountings will be ordinarily faint and then become more severe as more data is located. The data will finally be in a more or less complete state and the engram will begin to lift, rising up through the various tones. All prenatals are apathy experiences and are therefore serious.

67

Minor taps and discomforts in the womb are of no consequence. A true engram will consist of such a thing as a knitting needle being rammed through the fetus, half of the fetus' head being badly injured, blows of various kinds bringing about fetal unconsciousness and so forth. Return eventually will find an opening into any period when there has been pain.

Disbeliefs and antagonisms from the preclear on the subject of such a thing as an attempted abortion should be overlooked by the auditor or taken into account as the sign of an existing engram. A case is recalled wherein a girl insisted that if an abortion had ever been attempted on her it should have been successful. Through several sessions, while an attempt was made to lift birth, she continued this assertion until the auditor realized that this was probably a remark made by the abortionist (or the mother) when his efforts failed. As soon as this was suggested to the girl she was able to contact the actual incident. A chronic apathy case under treatment for some years in an institution, she suddenly responded to auditing, brought the abortion to tone 4, erased birth to tone 4 and recovered mentally and physically into a social asset well above normal.

The auditor should continue to suspect prenatals as long as he cannot get later engrams easily into tone 4. Once an engramic chain has been lifted at its end nearest to conception, the preclear should begin to release relatively automatically, aided but little by the auditor. The erasure should be in terms of laughter at its optimum. This laughter is the reversing of charges residual in the locks which depended for their fear content or antagonistic content upon the basic engrams.

Abortion attempts are easy to recognize when an auditor has had some experience. The parent who attempted the abortion will, after the child's birth, likely be a source of anxiety to the individual who seems to require a great deal of affection and at-

68 traction from that parent. The individual will be found to be most fond of the parent (or other) who did not aid, or who actually tried to prevent the abortion attempt. At this time abortion attempts are extremely common.

When an abortion attempt has been lifted, the engramic chain should easily be brought to the time track and exhausted.

Auditing is essentially very simple but it demands precise understanding of the principles involved and imagination and sympathy on the part of the auditor. He must learn to compute engramically—or learn to think with his analytical mind, only for the purposes of auditing others, engramically. His biggest problem is the discovery of the basic of basics. It may elude him for a considerable period of time.

There is, however, preparatory work to do in a case other than the discovery of the basic. Occasionally an entire time track must be rehabilitated in which "do not remember" and "can't remember" have obscured the track. Later locks can be found and exhausted in the same manner that engrams are exhausted, and rapid scanning methods may be developed in the future for these. The hysteria or fear of the individual can be momentarily allayed one way or the other and the problem of reaching the basic can be entered upon. There are as many types of case as there are cases, but these are the primary fundamentals.

An auditor must think his way through every case, taking as his data the constantly reiterated[10] statements of the preclear

---

10.   reiterate: to repeat (something done or said); say or do again or repeatedly.

during auditing, and accumulating experience as to how incidents can be thrust off the time track, burying them from sight by the analytical mind, thus forming a reactive mind to the detriment[11] of the organism.　　　　　　　　　　　　　　　　　　　　□

69

11.　detriment: 1. loss, damage, disadvantage or injury.

CHAPTER THIRTEEN

Exhaustion
of Engrams

The technique of exhausting an engram is not com-
plicated but it must be adhered to. An engram is an unconscious
moment containing physical pain and conceived or actual antagonism to the organism. Therefore, that engram before it is discovered
will exhibit antagonism toward the auditor trying to discover it.
When it is first discovered, it may be found to be lacking in its
essential data. There are many techniques by which this data can be
developed. In a prenatal engram the analytical mind apparently
must redevelop the situation. Many returns through the incident
are therefore necessary.

When an engram will not exhaust, the first thing the
auditor should suspect is an earlier engram. It is actually possible for
a later one to contain essential information which will not permit the
information to rise. In the course of auditing, when an engram is
restimulated by the auditor but will not rise above apathy and does
not seem to contain all the necessary data, the auditor must look for
an earlier engram, and it almost inevitably will be found to exist.
This precursor is then developed as the basic engram. If it follows the
same behavior pattern of not lifting or becoming complete, another
previous to it must be discovered. If at last the auditor is entirely
certain that there is no engram ahead of the one being run, some
possible locking mechanism later on may be found and exhausted, at
which time the basic may show itself. Continual application of energy
to the basic will at length bring it into full view and continual
recountings of it will gradually develop it, raise its tone and lift it into
tone 4.

The principle of recounting is very simple. The preclear is merely told to go back to the beginning and to tell it all over again. He does this many times. As he does it the engram should lift in tone on each recounting. It may lose some of its data and gain other. If the preclear is recounting in the same words time after time, it is certain that he is playing a memory record of what he has told you before. He must then be sent immediately back to the actual engram and the somatics of it restimulated. He will then be found to somewhat vary his story. He must be returned to the consciousness of somatics continually until these are fully developed, begin to lighten and are then gone. Tone 4 will appear shortly afterwards. If the preclear is bored with the incident and refuses to go on with it, there is either an earlier engram or there is other data in the engram which has not been located.

The auditor will discover that occasionally an engram when lifted into a 3, or even erased, without reaching laughter, will sag. This is a certain sign of an earlier basic on that chain. Any kind of sag from a tone 4 is impossible if tone 4 has truly been reached. Tone 4 will not be reached if there are earlier basics. The engram may vanish and be erased, but there will be no cheerfulness or laughter about it at the end if it is not the basic.

Once the basic has been reached and brought into tone 4, it will disappear. The next engram on the chain will be located and rather easily brought into tone 4. If one is accidentally skipped, the third in line will be found to hold or sag. The intermediate must then be located and brought into a tone 4. In such a way the chain will gradually come up into a complete tone 4. At this time the locks, the merely mentally painful incidents in the person's life, will begin to release automatically. These will erase or lift without any attention from the auditor. While these are releasing, the auditor must concern himself with secondary engrams.[1] These would be engrams on their own if they had not had forerunners. They therefore do not relieve after the removal of the basic but must be located as themselves. These in turn will start a chain of releasing locks which again need no attention. There may be entirely distinct engramic chains in the reactive mind which are not appended in any way to the original basic.

---

1.   secondary engram: painful emotion engram, similar to other engrams, it is caused by the shock of sudden loss such as the death of a loved one.

So long as a preclear retains any part of a reactive mind, he will be interested in himself (in the condition of his mind) and be introverted. Therefore, so long as he is interested in his own reactive mind, he is impeded in his dynamic pursuit of survival. A guarantee of a tone four is the patient's interest in positive action along his dynamics and his application of himself to the world around him. Introversion is not natural nor is it necessary to the creation of anything. It is a manifestation of the analytical mind trying to solve problems on improper data, and observing the organism being engaged in activities which are not conducive to survival along the dynamics. When a Clear has been reached, the basic personality and self-determinism of the individual will have asserted itself. No chronic somatics in the present will remain (excepting those which can be accounted for by actual disease, injury or malconstruction of the brain).

73

Though more germane[2] to Child Dianetics, it is of help to the auditor to know that a child can be considered to have formed his general basic purpose in life somewhere around the age of two. This purpose is fairly reliable, as at that time his engrams have probably not gained much force over him since his responsibilities are slight. He will have tried to hold his main purpose throughout his life but it will undoubtedly have been warped both by his reactive mind's experience content and by his environment. The time when the purpose is formed varies and may indeed never have manifested, as in the case of amentia.[3] As the preclear is normally interested in this purpose and its rehabilitation, he will often take a more intense interest in auditing if there is an attempt made to discover it. This purpose is quite valid and the preclear can be expected to rehabilitate his life along its dictates unless he is too oppressed by his environment. (It can be remarked that a Release or Clear will ordinarily order or change his environment.)

Vocational therapies have as their source the tenet of the rehabilitation of the general purpose of an individual or the establishment of a false purpose in order to allay the activity of his reactive mind. It has little bearing on Dianetics, but an auditor, for the term of auditing, may engage his preclear along the purpose line of

---

2.   germane: 1. truly relevant; pertinent; to the point.
3.   amentia: condition of feeblemindedness or mental deficiency.

becoming a Clear. This is not necessary and is indeed often automatic since the basic personality beholds at last a chance to manifest itself. However, it will occasionally aid the auditor.

The auditor should be prepared to have to solve many individual problems since above these basics are almost as many problems as there are cases. For example, in the case of a preclear who has several very nasty prenatals it will be found that the formation of the body in the womb has overlaid or confused the time track so that a later prenatal must be partially lifted before an earlier prenatal can be exhausted. This is often true of a later period of life. In one case an entire series of prenatals was held down by a dental operation under nitrous oxide at the age of twenty-five. Until some portion of this was removed, the bulk of the prenatals were not available. In short, the circuits of the mind can become entangled to a point where even the motor control time track is confused.

Dispersal of purpose by some engram along some dynamic or purpose line is a common situation and is indeed the basic concept. As a stream of electrons[4] would behave if they were to encounter a solid object in their path, so does a drive or purpose disperse. These many varied and faint tracks after impact with the engram are symptomatic. Along dynamic two, the sexual drive, promiscuity[5] inevitably and invariably indicates a sexual engram of great magnitude. Once that engram is removed promiscuity can be expected to cease.

Anxiety is established in the preclear's mind by such dispersals and he dramatizes because of the dispersal. This is one of the manifestations of his malady. No pervert ever became a pervert without having been educated or abused by a pervert. And that abuse must have been very thorough. The contagion[6] of engrams is an interesting manifestation which the auditor should and must observe. It can be said that insanity runs in families, not because this is a eugenic[7] truth but because a standard patter[8] during emergencies or stress creates certain types of engrams which in turn create types of

---

4.   electron: a particle of matter with a negative electric charge.
5.   promiscuous: 2. having sexual relations with many people.
6.   contagion: communication or transfer from one to another.
7.   eugenic: A. pertaining or adapted to the production of fine offspring especially in the human race.
8.   patter: special language or jargon.

insanities. Insanities are so definitely contagious that when a child is raised by aberrated parents, the child becomes aberrated. As would be delineated by Child Dianetics, the best way to guarantee a sane child is to provide it with cleared or released parents. This is of definite interest to the auditor since he will discover that in cases of severe prenatals and birth the engrams were also received by the mother exactly as they were received by the child. The child will thereafter be a restimulator to the mother and the mother a re-stimulator to the child for the severe incidents. The mother, having received the exact wording of the engram, also contains the engram. Restimulation by the child will occasion the use of the engramic language toward the child. This brings the infant and child and adolescent into the unhappy situation of having his birth engram or his prenatal engrams continually restimulated. This occasions dire[9] results and very great unhappiness in the home and is one of the main sources of family difficulties.

75

A child, even if he despises them, will dramatize the actions of his parents when he himself is married and when he himself has children. In addition to this the other partner in the marriage also has his or her own engrams. Their engrams combine into doubled engrams in the children. The result of this is a contagion and a progression of aberration. Thus any society which does not have a high purpose finds itself declining and gaining greater num-bers of insane. The contagion of aberration is at work progressively and the children become progressively aberrated until at last the society itself is aberrated.

While the fate of society belongs definitely in Social and Political Dianetics, the auditor is interested in the fact that he can take the prenatal and birth content of the engrams of his preclear and run them to discover postbirth locks and secondary engrams. The mother will normally have used much the same data whenever the troubles of the child impinged upon her reactive mind; this of course accounts for the locks.

The auditor will also discover that where he has a married preclear who is aberrated, he should have two preclears, which is to say, the partner. It is useless to return a preclear to his or her

---

9.   dire: 1. dreadful, terrible.

aberrated spouse and expect domestic tranquility to result. While the Release cannot and will not pick up his old engrams from the spouse in whom he has implanted them, he will, nevertheless, find his life made unbearable by the mere existence of a spouse that he himself may have aberrated.

Further, the children of these people will also need auditing, since they will be found (if the parents' aberrations were of any magnitude) to be sickly or aberrated or deficient in some way. The auditor should therefore, when he undertakes a case, be prepared to audit the family of his preclear, should an investigation of that preclear make it seem necessary.

Aberrations are contagious and where a person has been aberrated, his environment will to some degree also have become aberrated. The preclear may, for one thing, be somewhat victimized and impeded by his reactive mind which is now existing in his associates.

The auditor should not permit such terms as *psychoneurotic,*[10] *crazy* or *mentally exhausted* to exist for long in the preclear's mind. These are depressive and are actually aberrations in the society. It is true and provable that the preclear is on his way to being, not a person who is crazy or neurotic, but an individual who will have more stability and self-command and ability, possibly, than those around him. To be blunt: This is not the process of reviving corpses into a semblance of life. It is a process which, at its best usage, is taking the "normal" and "average" and giving them their birthright of happiness and creative attainment in the world of man. □

76

---

10.   psychoneurotic: neurotic: a person who is mainly harmful to himself by reason of his aberrations, but not to the point of suicide.

CHAPTER FOURTEEN

Engram Chains

More than one engramic chain will be found in every aberree. When this person becomes a preclear the dianeticist does well to discover the earliest chain. It is not always possible to do this with accuracy since a preclear is sometimes in such a nervous condition that he cannot be worked on his basic chain but must be alleviated in a greater or lesser degree by the exhaustion of a later and more available chain. This last, however, is not the usual case.

The dianeticist should clearly understand certain working principles and definitions. By an engram is meant a moment of unconsciousness accompanied by physical pain and conceived antagonism. The basic engram is the earliest engram on an engram chain. Also there may be engrams of the same character and kind on the same drive line as the basic engram of the chain. An engram chain is composed of a basic engram and a series of similar incidents. Engram chains also contain locks which are instances of mental anguish more or less known to the analytical mind. These are often mistaken by the preclear for the cause of his conduct. A true engram is unknown to the conscious computer of the preclear but underlies it as a false datum on which are erected almost equally unknown similar incidents and an enormous number of locks.

In order to release an engram chain it is vital and absolutely necessary to discover the basic of that chain. An individual will have more than one engram chain but he has a basic chain. This must be released as soon as possible after auditing is begun on the preclear.

When an engram is discovered by the dianeticist, he must examine the aspect of it to determine whether or not it is the basic. Discovering it is not, he must immediately determine an earlier basic, and so forth until he is obviously on the scene of the basic engram.

There are certain tests which he can apply. A basic engram will rise to laughter, sag slightly, and then rise to tone 4 and vanish. Successive engrams will then erase from that chain with very little work. Almost any engram on an engram chain can be exhausted, but if it is not a basic engram it will recede and vanish at times but will rise in part again when the basic engram has been reached and the preclear is brought forward into its area.

78

An engram not basic is subject to sag. Which is to say that it may be brought to the two point zero (2.0) tone, but after a certain length of time has elapsed—from one to two days—it will be found to have sagged and to be, for instance, in a one point one (1.1) tone. It can be successively lifted until it is apparently in a three point zero (3.0) tone, at which point much of its content will disappear. This is reduction.

Any engram chain can be reduced to some degree without reaching the basic but when it has been reached, the basic itself and subsequent engrams can be brought rapidly to tone 4 providing no engrams are skipped on the return up the time track.

When an engram chain has been brought to tone 4, it can be considered to have vanished. The preclear can no longer find it on the time track (he may even be unable to recall some of its most painful and disheartening aspects). The mind apparently has been proofed against the data it has contained. A search for an engram chain after it has been exhausted and a tone 4 has been achieved should, for purposes of auditing, be entirely fruitless.

Once the basic has been discovered and the engram chain has been brought to tone 4 the locks will vanish of their own accord. If this does not occur then there is something remaining or the auditor has been too optimistic about the selection of his basic engram for the chain and has not, in reality, discovered it.

All engram chains should be exhausted from a preclear. These may be discovered to lie along the various dynamics but any chain may influence more than one dynamic.

Another type of engram is the cross engram. This is usually a childhood or adult engram which embraces more than one engram chain. The receipt of the cross engram, containing as it does the convergence of two or more engram chains, is often accompanied by a "nervous breakdown" or the sudden insanity of an individual. A cross engram may occur in a severe accident, in prolonged or severe illness under antagonistic circumstances or a nitrous oxide operation. Cross engrams are very easy to locate but should not be addressed by the dianeticist as such since an enormous amount of work upon them will not exhaust them until the basic and the chains on which the cross engram depends have been brought to tone 4.

Postbattle neurasthenia[1] is almost always traceable to the receipt of a cross engram. This must be, of course, an engram in its own right on more than one chain. It is conceivable that it may be so severe that it "breaks" the individual even if it lies on only one chain.

There are certain rules the dianeticist may employ to establish the basic engram of a chain. In first entering a case these rules apply as well to the first goal which is the location of the basic engram of the basic chain.

Number one: No engram will lift if the basic of that chain has not been lifted.

Number two: The basic engram will not lift until the basic instant of the basic engram has been reached, which is to say, the first moment of the engram. Ordinarily this is the most obscure.

Number three: If after two or three test recountings of an engram it does not seem to be improving, the auditor should attempt to discover an earlier engram.

---

1.   neurasthenia: a type of neurosis . . . characterized by irritability, fatigue, weakness, anxiety and, often, localized pains or distress without apparent physical causes: formerly thought to result from weakness or exhaustion of the nervous system.

Number four: No engram is valid unless accompanied by somatic pain. This may be mild. Incidents which do not contain somatics are either not basic (the chain having been suspended by some such command as "can't feel" in the basic) or else it may not even be an engram.

Cases should be entered as near as possible to the basic engram. Then they should be returned to earlier incidents until the basic is discovered.

The running of locks themselves may accomplish some alleviation of a case. □

CHAPTER FIFTEEN

Prenatal, Birth and Infant Engrams

The human mind and the human anatomy are enor-
mously more powerful and resilient[1] than has commonly been supposed. Only incidents of the greatest magnitude in physical pain
and hostile content are sufficient to aberrate a mind.

The ability of the mind to store data can scarcely be
overrated. In early life before sound is analyzed as speech a human
being receives and stores exact impressions of everything which
occurs. At some future date, when similar perceptics are encountered,
the reactive mind reanalyzes—on the basis of identities only—the
content of the early mind. This becomes the foundation of the
postconception personality. The actual personality in the individual is
powerful and very difficult to aberrate. Unlike animals, which can be
driven mad by minor mechanisms of experimental psychology, a man
must be most severely handled before he begins to show any signs of
derangement. That derangement proceeds from the ability of the
reactive mind to store perceptions from the earliest moments of
existence and retain them on either the analytical or the reactive
plane for future reference.

The basic personality does not proceed from engrams and
the dynamics of the individual are impeded, not enhanced, by
engrams. The dynamics are entirely separate and are as native to the
individual as his basic personality, of which they are a part.

Information falls into two categories: the educational or
experience level, banked and available to the analytical mind on at
least its deeper levels; and aberrational, or data stored in the reactive

---

1.   resilient: 3. recovering readily from illness, depression, adversity or the like.

mind and often used but never reached by the analytical mind, save through auditing.

There would seem to be two types of recording. The first is cellular recording in which the cells would seem to store data. In that cells in procreating become themselves again—which is to say that when cell A divides, both halves are still cell A—cellular intelligence is not lost. Personal identity is duplicated. In the case of individual men, procreation is far more complex and individual identity is lost—the son is not the father but a genetic[2] composite of vast numbers of ancestors.

The cells of the human being shortly after conception are capable of enormous perceptic and retentive power. After a very short time in the womb, the brain and nervous system are already operating. From then until birth the human being is apparently capable of computations of a rather complex nature on the analytical mind level. Far more certainly he retains information on the reactive level.

Fear, pain and unconsciousness extend the range of perception of the individual. When the human being in the womb is injured his senses extend so as to record sounds outside the mother's body. He records them so well that their precise nature is stored for future reference. The human being in the womb responds exactly as it does after birth to the receipt of engrams, storing the data with precision and reacting to it.

The repair facilities available to a human being before birth are greatly enhanced by the presence of ample connective tissue,[3] oxygen and sustenance.[4] These repair facilities are unimaginably great so that a prenatal human being can be severely torn and ripped without becoming structurally deficient. It does, however, receive engrams and these are subject to restimulation. In many cases of attempted abortions it was found that large sections of the prenatal human being's brain could apparently be injured without the brain being deficient or even scarred after birth. These

---

2.   genetic: genetic applies to the . . . line of father and mother to child, grown child to new child and so forth.

3.   connective tissue: tissue found throughout the body, serving to bind together and support other tissues and organs.

4.   sustenance: 2. the food itself, nourishment.

repair facilities do not however lessen the extreme severity of the engrams which can be received by the prenatal human being. The word *fetus* is dropped at this point and it is advised that it should be dropped from the language as a description of a prebirth human being. Insufficient evidence is at hand to make an outright declaration that attempted abortions are responsible for the bulk of our criminal and insane aberrees. But according to the cases at hand the attempted abortion must be accounted responsible for the majority.

The attempted abortion is the most serious aberration producer. So exact is the recording of the prebirth human being that the reactive mind makes no errors in recognizing its enemies after birth. The mind becomes aberrated in having to depend upon these same enemies for the ordinary sustenance of life while the child is a helpless infant.

83

The diagnosis of a prenatal case is relatively simple. Nearly all preclears will be found to have at least one prenatal engram and the case will not solve unless that prenatal is reached and exhausted.

The dianeticist can usually establish the attempted abortion preclear by an investigation of the conduct of the infant and child. Uneasiness or unhappiness in the home, a feeling of not being wanted, unreasonable fear and a strong attachment to grandparents or another nonparental member of the household are often signs of an attempted abortion. Fear of the dark is usually but not always a part of the attempted abortion case. The auditor should suspect an abortion attempt in every preclear he audits, at least for this next generation. Whether or not the preclear disbelieves the diagnosis is of no importance to the auditor as the prenatal engrams may very well contain the words "can't believe it." The parents themselves, as well as society, mislead the individual as to the enormous prevalence[5] of this practice at this time.

The attempted abortion preclear may not be discovered to be such until considerable auditing has already been done. Any auditing done on an attempted abortion preclear, unless it is solely

---

5.   prevalence: 1. widespread; of wide extent or occurrence; in general use or acceptance.

addressed to making the case workable, is wasted until the attempted abortions are reached.

The postbirth aberree presents a somewhat different case than the prenatal since his case can be entered at any point and the earliest moments of it can be attained easily. This is not true of the attempted abortion preclear. Attempted abortions may run to any number. Since they are easily the most prevalent dramatization of engrams in the society, they are repeated time and again. The auditor will find it necessary to "unstack" the prenatal period. He will ordinarily reach the latest prenatal injury first. As he finds and examines it, it places itself on the time track. By going to earlier and earlier attempts, more and more of these engrams are revealed until at last the earliest is discovered. The auditor must be prepared to spend many hours of hard work in unstacking injuries. He will many times believe that he has reached the basic of that engram chain only to discover that another type of abortion was attempted prior to that moment. He need not address these engrams for any length of time before he goes on to the earlier one. He should only get some idea of them so that they will be easily locatable on the return. The basic engram on the attempted abortion case may be found shortly after the first missed period of the mother.

Its emotion will be exactly that of the person or persons attempting to perform the abortion. The prenatal human being identifies himself with himself but an adult returned to the prenatal period is reinterpreting the data and will find that he has and is confusing himself with other people associated in the attempts. This engramic data may have slumbered for years before it became violently restimulated and may indeed never have been awakened. It must be removed, however, before a Release can be obtained. The auditor should be prepared to unstack fifty or more incidents before birth if necessary.

When he is at last in the vicinity of the basic, even the most skeptical preclear (one who has skepticism as part of the prenatal engram chains) will have no further question as to what is happening to him. The auditor should be prepared to encounter difficulty in the ability of the preclear to hear voices or feel pain, as it is quite common for the engramic content to contain such phrases as "unconscious" and "can't see, can't feel, can't hear," this having been the misconception of the society regarding prenatal life.

The auditor should never be appalled at the damage the prenatal human being has received and so question the validity of his preclear's data. Unless the umbilical cord[6] is severed or the heart is stopped it is apparently the case that no damage, particularly in the earlier months, is too great for the organism to reconstruct.

In that parents performing abortions are usually drama- tizing attempted abortions which have been performed on them, rationality of content in the engrams should not be expected. Even the data given for it by the abortionist father, mother or professional is often entirely inaccurate.

85

The test of an engram is whether or not it will lift and whether or not the somatics which accompanied it disappear and a tone 4 is obtained. Rearranging data into other sequences will not obtain this. The exact content must be brought out.

The attempted abortion human being is often struck un- conscious by the earliest part of each attempt since the head is so available to the knitting needles, hat pins, orangewood sticks, buttonhooks and so forth which are employed. These periods of unconsciousness must be penetrated and will quite ordinarily release slowly.

The number of prenatal engrams should not particularly appall the auditor for when the basic has been discovered and a tone 4 achieved, the succeeding experiences will lift with greater and greater ease. The periods of consciousness interspersed between the prenatal engrams, being locks, will vanish.

Birth is in itself a severe experience and is recorded by the human being from the first moments of pain throughout the entire experience. Everything in a birth is engramic since the human being conceives the ministrations[7] to be more or less antagonistic when

---

6.   umbilical cord: cord connected to the navel of the fetus to supply nourishment prior to birth.
7.   ministration: 2. the act or an instance of giving help or care; service.

they are accompanied by so much pain. A birth must be lifted as a matter of course but not until the presence or absence of prenatals has been established. Even after birth has been lifted, prenatals should be looked for, since prenatals may often be found only after birth has been exhausted. The habits of obstetricians,[8] the presence of sound and speech in the delivery room, the swabbing of an infant's nostrils, the examination of its mouth, the severe treatment administered to start its breathing and the drops on the eyes may account in themselves for many psychosomatic ills. A cough, however, although it is present in birth and seems to be alleviated by the exhaustion of the birth engram, is quite ordinarily blood running down the throat of the prenatal during an attempted abortion. Any perception during birth, when difficulty is encountered with breathing, may become a restimulator for asthma.[9] Clean fresh air and electric lights may cause allergies and may be the principal restimulators. Everything said during birth, as well as everything said during prenatal experiences, is recorded in the reactive mind and acts as aberrational matter which can and does cause psychological and physiological changes in the individual. Because the parents are not greatly in evidence at birth, this experience may not be restimulated for many years. Prenatals, on the other hand, restimulate more easily.

86

Infant life is very sentient.[10] Delay in learning to talk is delay in learning the complexity of handling vocal muscles rather than an inability to record. Everything in infant life is recorded and the engrams received in it are extremely valid.

The auditor will find himself dealing mainly with prenatal, birth and infant life. The cases are very rare which have many important basics in childhood or adult life. These last periods contain mainly other engrams which, though they must be addressed to create the Release, should not engage much initial attention on the part of the dianeticist. Most of the experiences of mental anguish in childhood and adult life are founded on very early engrams and are locks which are almost self-removing.

---

8.   obstetrician: a medical doctor who specializes in obstetrics (the branch of medicine concerned with the care and treatment of women during pregnancy, childbirth and the period immediately following).

9.   asthma: a chronic disorder characterized by wheezing, coughing, difficulty in breathing and a suffocating feeling.

10.   sentient: of, having or capable of feeling or perception; conscious.

Moments of unconsciousness which contain physical pain and conceived antagonism lying in childhood and adult life are serious and can produce aberration. Engram chains complete with basic may be found which will, all by themselves, exhaust.   □

CHAPTER SIXTEEN

The "Laws" of Returning

By aberration is meant the aberree's reactions to and difficulties with his current environment.

By somatic is meant any physical or physically sensory abnormality which the preclear manifests generally or sporadically in his environment, or any such manifestation encountered and reexperienced during auditing.

The aberration is the mental error caused by engrams and the somatic is the physical error occasioned by the same source.

The auditor follows the general rule that no aberrations or somatics exist in a subject which cannot be accounted for by engrams. He may ordinarily be expected to discover that anything which reduces the physical or mental perfection of the subject is engramic. He applies this rule first and in practice admits no organic trouble of any character. Only when he has obviously obtained a Clear and when he has observed and has had that Clear medically examined after a period of sixty days to six months from the end of auditing should he be content to assign anything to organic origin. He cannot be expected to know until the final examination exactly what somatic was not engramic. In other words he must persistently adhere to one line of thought (that the preclear can be brought to mental and physical perfection) before he resigns any mental or physical error in the preclear to a purely organic category. Too little is known at this writing of the recoverability of the mind and body for a dianeticist to deny that ability to recover. Since primary research, considerable practice has demonstrated that this ability to reconstruct and recover is enormous, far beyond anything previously conceived possible.

Dianetics accounts for *all* faith healing phenomena on an entirely scientific basis and the dianeticist can expect himself to consort[1] daily in his practice with what appear to be miracles.

In addition to knowledge of his subject, considerable intelligence and imagination, and a personality which inspires confidence, the Dianetic auditor must possess persistency to a remarkable degree. In other words, his drives must be phenomenally high. There is no substitute for the auditor's having been cleared. It is possible for an individual to operate with Dianetics without having been released and he may do so for some time without repercussion, but as he audits he will most certainly encounter the perceptics contained in some of his own engrams time after time until these engrams are so restimulated that he will become mentally or physically ill.

In psychoanalysis[2] it was possible for the analyst to escape this fate because he dealt primarily with locks occurring in the postspeech life. The analyst might even experience relief from operating on patients since it might clarify his own locks which always had been more or less completely available to his analytical mind. This is very far from the case with the dianeticist who handles continually the vital and highly charged data which *cause* physical and mental aberrations. An auditor in Dianetics may work with impunity[3] for a very short time only before his own condition demands that he himself be audited. While this is aside from the main subject of auditing, it has been too often observed to be neglected.

Every engram possesses some quality which denies it to the analytical mind. There are several types. First there is the *denyer* engram which contains the species of phrase "Frank will never know about this," "forget it!" "cannot remember it!" and so forth. Second is the *self-invalidating* engram which contains the phrases "never

---

1.   consort: 1. to keep company; associate.
2.   psychoanalysis: method of mental therapy developed by Sigmund Freud in 1894.
3.   impunity: exemption from punishment, penalty or harm.

happened," "can't believe it," "wouldn't possibly imagine it" and so on.

Third is the *bouncer* engram which contains the species of phrase "can't stay here," "get out!" and other phrases which will not permit the preclear to remain in its vicinity but return him to present time. A fourth is the *holder* engram which contains "stay here," "hold still," "can't get out" and so on.

These are four of the general types which the dianeticist will find occasion him the greatest difficulty. The type of phrase being encountered, however, is easily diagnosed from preclear reaction.

91

There are many other types of engrams and phrases which will be encountered. There is the *self-perpetuating* engram which implies that "It will always be this way" and "It happens all the time." The auditor will soon learn to recognize them, forming lists of his own.

An engram would not be an engram unless it had strong compulsive or repressive data contained in it. All engrams are self-locking to some degree, being well off the time track and touching it slightly, if at all, with some minor and apparently innocuous[4] bit of information which the analytical mind disregards as unimportant. Classed with the denyer variety are those phrases which deny perception of any kind. The Dianetic auditor will continually encounter perception denial and will find it one of the primary reasons the preclear cannot recall and articulate[5] the engram. "Can't see," "can't hear," "can't feel" and "isn't alive" tend to deny the whole engram containing any such phrases.

As the engram is a powerful surcharge of physical pain, it will without any phrases whatsoever deny itself to the analytical mind which, in seeking to scan the engram, is repelled by the operating principle that it must avoid pain for the organism. As has already been covered, there are five ways the organism can handle a source of pain. It can neglect it, attack it, succumb to it, flee from it or avoid it. As the entire organism handles exterior pain sources, so does

---

4.   innocuous: 1. that does not injure or harm; harmless.
5.   articulate: 4. to express clearly.

the analytical mind tend to react to engrams. Everything contained in the reactive mind is exterior source material. The analytical mind was out of circuit and was recording imperfectly if at all in the time period when the exterior source was entered into the reactive mind.

An analytical mind when asked to approach an engram reacts as it would have had it been present, which is to say, in circuit, at the moment when the engram was being received. It tends to go out of the circuit. Therefore, an artificial approach to the engram must be made which will permit the auditor to direct the subject's analytical mind into but one source of action: Attack.

The actual incident must be located and reexperienced. In that the analytical mind has five possible ways of reacting to the engram and in that the auditor desires that only one of these—attack—be used, the preclear must be persuaded from using the remaining four.

On this general principle can be created many types of approach to the problem of obtaining a Clear. The one which is offered in this manual is that one which has met with quicker and more predictable results than others researched at this time. It has given, in use, one hundred percent results. In the beginning, at this time, an auditor should not attempt to stray far from this offered technique. He should attempt to vary it only when he himself has had extensive and sufficient practice which will enable him to be very conversant with the nature of engrams. Better techniques will undoubtedly be established which will provide swifter exhaustion of the reactive mind. The offered technique has produced results in all types of cases so far encountered.

There are three equations which demonstrate how and why the auditor and preclear can reach engrams and exhaust them:

I. The auditor's dynamics are equal to or less than the engramic surcharge in the preclear.

II. The preclear's dynamics are less than the engramic surcharge.

III. The auditor's dynamics plus the preclear's dynamics are greater than the engramic surcharge.

When the preclear's dynamics are entirely or almost entirely reduced, as in the case of amnesia trance, drug trances and so forth, the auditor's dynamics are not always sufficient to force the preclear's analytical mind into an attack upon the engram.

The auditor's dynamics directed against an engram in a preclear who has not been subjected to a process which will inhibit the free play of his reactive mind and concentrate it, ordinarily provokes the preclear into one of the four unusable methods of succumbing, fleeing, avoiding or neglecting the engram. Demanding that the preclear "face reality" or "see reason" or that he "stop his foolish actions" fall precisely into this category. The auditor's dynamics operating against an awake preclear can produce an "insanity break," temporary or of considerable duration in the preclear.

When the preclear is in reverie some of his own dynamics are present and the auditor's dynamics added to these make a combination sufficient to overcome the engramic surcharge.

If the auditor releases his dynamics *against* the analytical mind of the preclear, which is to say, the person of the preclear, while an attempt is being made to reach an engram (in violation of the Auditor's Code or with some erroneous idea that the whole person of the preclear is confronting him) he will receive in return all the fury of the engramic surcharge.

An engram can be dramatized innumerable times, for such is the character of the reactive mind that the surcharge of the engram cannot exhaust itself and will not exhaust itself regardless of its age or the number of times dramatized until it has been approached by the analytical mind of the subject.

The additive dynamic drive law must be made to apply before engrams are reached. It is occasionally very necessary to change Dianetic auditors, for some preclears will work well only with either a male or a female auditor or with one or another individual auditor. This will not be found necessary in many cases. Three cases are on record where the preclear was definitely antipathetic toward the auditor throughout the entire course of auditing. The dianeticist was found to be a restimulator for one or more of the persons contained in the engrams. Even so, these persons responded. Greater patience was required on the part of the auditor. Closer observance of the Auditor's Code was necessary and a longer time was required for auditing. It will be discovered that once the preclear understands what is desired of him and why, his basic personality is aroused to the extent that it will cooperate with any auditor in order to be free. It will suffer through many violations of the Auditor's Code. Once a preclear has started his auditing he will ordinarily continue to cooperate in the major requirements to the fullest extent, no matter what apparent antagonisms he may display in minor matters.

94

Reverie is a method that has been used with success. The analytical mind of the preclear, while reduced in its potential and under direction, is still capable of thinking its own thoughts and forming its own opinions. Implicit[6] obedience to whatever the auditor suggests is not desirable as the preclear will inject extraneous material at the faintest suggestion of the auditor. Drugs inhibit the somatic and have no use in entering a case.

The fact that the dianeticist is interested solely in what has been done *to* the preclear and is not at all interested in what the preclear himself has done to others greatly facilitates auditing since there is no social disgrace in having been an unwitting victim.

In reverie the preclear is placed in a light state of "concentration" which is not to be confused with hypnosis. In the state of alliance,[7] therefore, the mind of the preclear will be found to be, to some degree, detachable from his surroundings and directed interiorly. The first thing that the dianeticist will discover in most preclears is aberration of the sense of time. There are various ways that he can circumvent this and construct a time track along which he can cause the preclear's mind to travel. Various early experiences which are easily reached are examined and an early diagnosis can be formed. Then begins an immediate effort to reach basic, with

---

6.   implicit: 3. without reservation or doubt; unquestioning; absolute.
7.   alliance: 5. a merging of efforts or interests by persons, families, states or organizations.

attempted abortion or prenatal accident predominating.[8] Failures on the first attempts to reach prenatal experiences should not discourage the Dianetic auditor since many hours may be consumed and many false basics reached and exhausted before the true prenatal basic is attained.

In this type of reverie the dianeticist can use and will observe certain apparently natural laws in force. They are as follows:

The difficulties the analytical mind encounters when returned to or searching for an engram are identical to the command content of that engram.

An aberree in adult life is more or less obeying, as restimulated, the composite experiences contained in his engrams.

The preclear's behavior in reverie is regulated by the commands contained in the engram to which he is returned and is modified by the composite of chronologically preceding engrams on his time track.

The somatics of a preclear are at their highest in an engram where they were received and at the moment of reception in that experience.

When returned to a point prior to an engram, the commands and somatics of that engram are not effective on the preclear. As he is returned to the moment of an engram, the preclear experiences, as the common denominator of all engrams, a considerable lessening of his analytical potential. He speaks and acts in a modified version of the engram. All complaints he makes to the auditor should be regarded as possibly being verbatim from, first, the engram that he is reexperiencing, or second, from prior engrams.

At the precise moment of an engramic command the preclear experiences obedience to that command. The emotion a preclear experiences when regressed to an engram is identical to the emotional tone of that engram. Excesses of emotion will be found to be contained in the word content of the engram as commands.

95

---

8.   predominate: 1. to be the stronger or leading element; prevail.

When a preclear is returned to before the moment of reception of an engram he is not subject to any part of that engram, emotionally, aberrationally or somatically.

When the time track is found to contain loops or is blurred in any portion, its crossings or confusions are directly attributable to engramic commands which precisely state the confusion.

Any difficulty a preclear may experience with returning, reaching engrams, perceiving or recounting, are directly and precisely commanded by engrams.

96

An engram would not be an engram were it easy to reach or if it gave the preclear no difficulty and contained no physical pain.

The characteristic of engrams is confusion. First, the confusion of the time track; second, the confusion of an engramic chain wherein similar words or somatics mix incidents; third, confusion of incidents with engrams.

This confusion is occasioned by the disconnected state of the analytical mind during the receipt of the engram. Auditing by location and identification of hidden incidents, first rebuilds at least the early part of the time track, locates and fixes engrams in relation to one another in time and then locates the basic of the basic chain and exhausts it. The remainder of the chain must also be exhausted. Other engrams and incidents exhaust with ease after the erasure of the basic or the basic of any chain (within that chain). Locks vanish without being located. A tone 4 gained on basic permits the subsequent erasure on the time track to go forward with ease. A whole chain may rise to 4 without the basic chain having been located.

Any perception of prespeech life during reverie denotes the existence of engramic experience as far back as the time track is open.

If the individual's general tone is clearly not tone 4, if he is still interested in his engrams, another more basic chain than the one found still exists.

Engramic patterns tend to form an avoidance pattern for the preclear. From basic outward there is an observable and progressive divergence[9] between the person himself and his returned self. In the basic engram of the basic chain and for a few subsequent incidents on that chain, he will be found within and receiving the experiences as himself. In subsequent incidents cleavage[10] is observable, and in late engrams the preclear is found to be observing the action from outside of himself, almost as a disinterested party. This forms the principal primary test for the basic of the basic chain. Another test for basic is sag.

Any engram may be exhausted to a point where it will recede without reaching tone 4. Although it is temporarily and momentarily lost to the individual and apparently does not trouble him, that engram which has been exhausted in a chain without the basic having been reached will sag or reappear within twenty-four to sixty hours. Basic on any chain will not sag but will lift on a number of recountings, rise to tone 4 and will remain erased. Another test for basic is whether or not it begins to lift with ease. If an engram does not intensify or remain static[11] after many recountings, it can be conceived to be at least a basic on some chain. Locks will lift and disappear without returning as they are not fixed by physical pain. Large numbers of locks can be exhausted bringing an alleviation of the preclear's difficulties and such a course may occasionally be pursued in the entrance of a case. The discovery and lifting of the basic to which the locks are appended removes the locks automatically.

These rules and laws, even if modified in their statement, will be found invariable. Incompetent auditing cannot be excused by the supposed discovery of a special case or exception. A physical derangement must be in the category of actually missing parts of the organism which cause permanent disability, and instances of this are not common.   □

---

9.   divergence: 2. a becoming different in form or kind.
10.   cleavage: 2. the state of being cleft (split; divided).
11.   static: 3. not changing.

CHAPTER SEVENTEEN

Case Histories

The following case histories have been selected at random. Due to lack of time, these case histories are Releases, not Clears. The Releases have been fully diagnosed and researched.

99

Case No. 1

Hypertension,[1] Combat Fatigue[2]
Tuberculosis,[3] Arrested
Myopic[4] Astigmatism[5]

A forty-three-year-old ex-army officer and author; inclined to petty tyrannies;[6] twice divorced; no children. Processed by army as psychoneurotic.

Birth was discovered immediately but would not satisfactorily release. The preclear experienced great difficulty in visualizing and his aberrations intensified during auditing.

By use of dreams and restimulation of somatics the preclear was able to reach the beginning of the engramic chain as counted backwards from birth. Fifteen prenatal experiences were unstacked. They were found lying in two loops. The loops were corrected and the basic engram of the basic chain was reached. (A loop is

---

1. hypertension: 2. abnormally high blood pressure, or a disease of which this is the chief sign.
2. combat fatigue: a mental disorder due to stress in wartime combat.
3. tuberculosis: an infectious disease that may affect almost any tissue of the body, especially the lungs.
4. myopic: nearsighted (seeing distinctly at a short distance only).
5. astigmatism: a defect in an eye or lens preventing proper focusing.
6. tyranny: 3a. oppressive, severe and unjust domination.

a redoubling of the time track back on itself. In this case incidents are not in their correct place on the time track.)

The basic consisted of a severe quarrel between his mother and father with several abdominal blows being received by the mother. The mother was protesting that it would make her sick all of her life. At the same time the mother was coughing from a throat blow. The father was insisting that he was master in his own home and that people had to do what he told them. This quarrel occurred at about 4½ months after conception and resulted in the temporary paralysis of the preclear's right side. The remainder of the chain consisted of similar incidents, evidently dramatizations on the part of the father of his own engrams, as the words used were almost identical, one engram to the next. This chain accounted for and relieved the subject's fear that he would be ill and his desire to tyrannize others.

Birth was then found to consist of near suffocation and considerable antagonism between the doctor and the nurse. This was registered as commands to himself to the effect that he was blind and could not see. Birth was in the home and dust, camphor, the smell of clean sheets and greased metal were the restimulators for this severe lung irritation. This birth was not restimulated until the age of five and the prenatals were not restimulated until entrance into the service when the need for authority manifested itself.

No locks were found to need attention and only one half hour of his war experience failed to release, that being a new basic.

Number of hours on case: fifty-five.

100

Case No. 2

Apathy, preclear had been under psychiatric treatment for two years prior to Dianetic auditing. She had experienced no relief. Malnutrition.

An eighteen-year-old girl in a condition of apathy bordering upon a break and worsening. She had been recently married. Afraid of her husband. She had done very badly in school, sporadically engaged in sexual escapades, relapsing afterwards into an illness which was variously diagnosed.

101

Case was entered with ease. Birth was reached and would not exhaust. A search for prenatals was for ten hours fruitless, until certain somatics were artificially restimulated and intensified to the point that the preclear had to recall the incident to find relief. Eight prenatals were then unstacked and only two incidents were discovered in confusion with each other, held together with a head somatic.

The basic proved to be a mutual abortion attempt by the mother and father. The mother said that she would die if anyone found out but that she would probably die anyway. The father said that the baby was probably like her and that he didn't want it. Eighteen penetrations of the head, throat and shoulders with a long orangewood stick—probably the third month. Several similar incidents completed this chain. Coitus followed each attempt at abortion. Another incident proved to be a basic without a chain and with innumerable locks: an attempted abortion by a professional abortionist who used some form of needle and scraper. Birth was found to be a mild experience. Three infant engrams with their own basic were discovered. They consisted of the mother's fear over the injury and the fear that the baby would die.

Contagion of attempted abortion engrams was particularly manifest in the mother's neurotic dwelling on fear of death, which was obviously a dramatization.

All neurotic and psychotic symptoms were relieved with a marked improvement in the health of the preclear and an increase of twenty-seven points on the Army Alpha test.[7]

Time of work: sixty-five hours.

Case No. 3

Psychotic murderous rages.
Chronic skin rash.

A thirty-year-old male negro, six feet four inches in height, about two hundred and fifty pounds—swamp worker. He was in continual trouble with police and had a considerable jail record. He continually dramatized a hatred of women. He also dramatized a continuous suspicion that he was about to be murdered. His IQ was about eighty-five.

Uniquely enough this case offered no difficulties in entrance. The subject was extremely cooperative with the dianeticist. Birth was found and exhausted without improvement in the case. A number of infant and childhood engrams were discovered and tested. Continual address of the preclear's attention to prenatal life finally brought about a convulsion[8] in which terror and rage alternated. The dianeticist was able to induce the preclear to listen to the voices he was hearing and to go through with the experience.

The convulsion proved to be twenty engrams nearer birth than the basic, which laid on another chain and which was discovered by dream technique. The convulsion was caused by the dramatization of an engram involving the injection of turpentine into the uterus by the mother in an attempted abortion. The main engramic chain consisted of the mother's efforts to abort herself. From engramic content it was gathered that the mother was a prostitute, for as many as twenty experiences of coitus succeeded two of these abortion attempts. They were too numerous to be evaluated.

---

7.   Army Alpha test: psychological test.
8.   convulsion: 1. a violent, involuntary contraction or spasm of the muscles.

The basic chain contained many quarrels about money between the mother and her customers. The somatics of this chain were largely bruises and concussions caused by the mother ramming herself into pointed objects or beating her stomach and abdomen. There were many loops in the basic chain caused by the similarity of incident and the confusion of coitus with abortion attempts. The basic incident was at last discovered and exhausted. It was found to lie about twenty days after conception, when the mother first discovered her pregnancy.

All engrams were exhausted in the basic chain. The convulsion was fully cleared and birth was suddenly found to have been a very painful experience, particularly because the child was taken by others immediately after birth. Only one engram chain (unconsciousness resulting from fist fights) was found in childhood.

103

☐

About
the Author

Whether introduced through the pages of one of his
589 published works, or through a direct personal encounter, L. Ron
Hubbard is a man once met, never forgotten. And while he has
become known for advances in a variety of fields, he is known by
millions as one of the foremost writers of self-betterment books
in the world today. His works on the subjects of Dianetics, human
relationships and life itself have sold over twenty-three million
copies.

L. Ron Hubbard's hallmark is that he writes with a purpose,
reads insatiably, researches meticulously and lives what he writes
about. Few are the writers that can appeal so well to so many with
a first-hand knowledge of the basics of life and ability.

Born in Tilden, Nebraska on March 13, 1911, Hubbard
spent his early years in Montana where he learned horsemanship
growing up with the last of the old frontiersmen and cowboys. An old
Indian medicine man was a best friend.

The son of a naval man, L. Ron Hubbard traveled to China,
Japan and the Pacific Islands. At only fifteen years of age, he traveled
far on his own into China and to Manchuria, encountering wide
variations in culture and custom in the peoples he met.

After returning to the United States, Hubbard completed
his schooling and supported himself while in college and in his
research by writing a wide variety of articles and stories. His perception of life quickly won him acclaim as he poured out literally
millions of words. He wrote aviation articles (he was also a glider

pilot and barnstormer), westerns, sports stories, sea stories, detective thrillers, military intrigues and adventure of every kind on every continent. Later he joined forces with one of the greatest editors of science fiction, John W. Campbell, Jr., and helped to launch what was later called "The Golden Age of Science Fiction."

In 1932, Hubbard was startled to find that the culture in which we live had no more workable knowledge of the mind than a Shaman of the Goldi people of Manchuria or a Blackfoot medicine man. Here was a society that was excelling in the physical sciences but had no means of bettering man's ability to live his life and secure his own sanity. He began research into the underlying principles of life to try to resolve some of the problems of mankind.

Hubbard continued to write to support himself in his research which included expeditions conducted to investigate primitive cultures. Between the years of 1933 and 1940, he conducted three expeditions that in 1940 earned him election to the prestigious Explorer's Club of New York.

Then, in 1941, the Second World War broke out. Following the war and deeply affected by his service in it, Hubbard continued his research. He began to synthesize what he had learned of Eastern philosophy, nuclear physics and scientific methodology and working with men in war.

Hubbard made breakthroughs and developed techniques that enabled his own recovery from his war experiences. He concluded that the results he was obtaining could help others to gain greater ability, health and happiness and it was during this period that the basic tenets of Dianetics were formed.

In 1948, L. Ron Hubbard wrote *The Dynamics of Life—An Introduction to Dianetics Discoveries.* This manuscript summarized the previously uncharted landscape of the human mind. Here was something completely new—a workable science of the mind that could produce results where others believed results were not possible.

This manuscript was copied and recopied and passed from hand to hand throughout the world.

The popularity of this work prompted publishers to contract for a popular work on the subject of Dianetics.

Dianetics: The Modern Science of Mental Health was then published in May 1950. Response to the book was positive and instantaneous. By late summer 1950, the book was high on the New York Times Best Seller lists. People across the United States were reading the book and using the techniques outlined in it to attain new levels of certainty and ability.

107

The tremendous public response to Dianetics created broad popular demand for the original work to be published as well. To meet this demand, *The Dynamics of Life—An Introduction to Dianetics Discoveries* was published in Wichita, Kansas in December 1951.

L. Ron Hubbard had little respect for the "official" treatments employed in the name of "mental health." And so he became a target for those who supported programs of psychosurgery, electric shock, drugs and hypnosis.

Undaunted, his research continued and still continues today.

Since these early days, L. Ron Hubbard has continued his research and written over fifty works on the subjects of philosophy, human relationships, self-betterment and Dianetics. He has also given more than 3,000 lectures on these subjects. These works represent a complete, fully detailed and workable technology of the mind and life.

With this technology it has become possible for men to truly become sane and confident in their abilities and handling of life.

L. Ron Hubbard's research and discoveries and his Dianetics technology have improved the lives of millions.

People all over the world consider they have no truer friend.   □

108   You can always write to L. Ron Hubbard:

I am always willing to help. By my own creed, a being is only as valuable as he can serve others.

Any message addressed to me and sent to the address of the nearest organization listed in the back of this book shall be given prompt and full attention in accordance with my wishes.

Glossary

Words of Dianetics that are footnoted have definitions developed by the author in his researches.

The numbers that appear in parentheses directly following the entry words of each definition indicate the page number where the word first appears in the text. The next number in a definition will be the number of that definition in the dictionary it was extracted from. It indicates that there are more definitions than are listed here.

abbreviate: (pg. 5) to shorten by cutting off a part; to cut short. —*Defn. 3. Oxford English Dictionary*

aberration(s): (pg. 3) a departure from rational thought or behavior. From the Latin, *aberrare*, to wander from; Latin, *ab*, away, *errare*, to wander. It means basically to err, to make mistakes, or more specifically to have fixed ideas which are not true. The word is also used in its scientific sense. It means a departure from a straight line. If a line should go from A to B, then if it is "aberrated" it would go from A to some other point, to some other point, to some other point, to some other point, to some other point and finally arrive at B. Taken in its scientific sense, it would also mean the lack of straightness or to see crookedly as, in example, a man sees a horse but thinks he sees an elephant. Aberrated conduct would be wrong conduct or conduct not supported by reason. When a person has engrams, these tend to deflect what would be his normal ability to perceive truth and bring about an aberrated view of situations which then would cause an aberrated reaction to them. Aberration is opposed to sanity, which would be its opposite.

aberree: (pg. 22) an aberrated person.

abyss: (pg. 9) anything too deep for measurement; profound depth. —*Defn. 2. Webster's New World Dictionary*

acute: (pg. 51) brief and severe. —*Defn. 4. Random House College Dictionary*

aggregation: (pg. 5) collection into an unorganized whole. —*Defn. 2. Random House College Dictionary*

allay(ed): (pg. 52) to lessen, relieve or alleviate. —*Defn. 2. Webster's New World Dictionary*

allergy(-gies): (pg. 55) a condition producing an unfavorable reaction to certain foods, pollens, etc. —*Oxford American Dictionary*

alliance: (pg. 94) a merging of efforts or interests by persons, families, states or organizations. —*Defn. 5. Random House College Dictionary*

amentia: (pg. 73) condition of feeblemindedness or mental deficiency. —*editor*

amnesia: (pg. 30) partial or total loss of memory caused by brain injury or by shock, repression, etc. —*Webster's New World Dictionary*

analogy: (pg. 11) an explaining of something by comparing it point by point with something similar. —*Defn. 2. Webster's New World Dictionary*

anatomy: (pg. 30) the structure of an animal or plant or any of its parts. —*Defn. 2. Random House College Dictionary*

antipathetic: (pg. 19) opposed or antagonistic in character, tendency, etc. —*Defn. 2. Webster's New World Dictionary*

approximation: (pg. 14) a coming or getting near to identity in quantity, quality or degree; an approach to a correct estimate or conception of anything. —*Defn. 3. Oxford English Dictionary*

Army Alpha test: (pg. 102) psychological test. —*editor*

articulate: (pg. 91) to express clearly. —*Defn. 4. Webster's New World Dictionary*

assists: (pg. 152) simple, easily done processes that can be applied to anyone to help them recover more rapidly from accidents, mild illness or upsets.

asthma: (pg. 86) a chronic disorder characterized by wheezing, coughing, difficulty in breathing and a suffocating feeling. —*Webster's New World Dictionary*

astigmatism: (pg. 99) a defect in an eye or lens preventing proper focusing. —*Oxford American Dictionary*

111

attendant(ly): (pg. 20) accompanying as a circumstance or result. —*Defn. 3. Webster's New World Dictionary*

attune(d): (pg. 14) to adjust; bring into accord, harmony or sympathetic relationship. —*Random House College Dictionary*

audio: (pg. 23) of hearing or sound. —*Webster's New World Dictionary*

auditing: (pg. 20) the application of Dianetics processes and procedures to someone by a trained auditor. Dianetics auditing includes as its basic principle the exhaustion of all the painfully unconscious moments of a subject's life.

auditor: (pg. 20) the individual who administers Dianetics procedures. To audit means "to listen" and also "to compute."

Auditor's Code: (pg. viii) the governing set of rules for the general activity of auditing.

auto-control: (pg. 45) autohypnosis used in Dianetics is probably as close to fruitless masochism as one can get. If a patient places himself in autohypnosis and regresses himself in an effort to reach illness or birth or prenatals, the only thing he will get is ill.

axioms: (pg. 1) statements of natural laws on the order of those of the physical sciences.

basic: (pg. 33) the first experience recorded in mental image pictures of that type of pain, sensation, discomfort, etc. Every chain has its basic. It is a peculiarity and a fact that when one gets down to the basic on a chain, (a) it erases and (b) the whole chain vanishes for good. Basic is simply earliest.

capricious(ly): (pg. 56) characterized by or subject to whim; impulsive and unpredictable. —*American Heritage Dictionary*

cathode ray tube: (pg. 66) a vacuum tube, for example, a television picture tube, in which beams of electrons are directed against a fluorescent screen where they produce a luminous image. —*Oxford American Dictionary*

chain: (pg. 27) a series of incidents of similar nature or similar subject matter.

charge: (pg. 24) electrical charge, the quantity of electricity or electrical energy in or upon an object or substance. —*Defn. 39a. Random House College Dictionary*

charlatan: (pg. 60) a person who pretends to knowledge or skill; quack. —*Random House College Dictionary*

Child Dianetics: (pg. 11) that branch of Dianetics which is concerned with promoting optimum survival of the immature human organism until such time as standard procedure for adults may be employed.

chronic: (pg. 35) affecting a person for a long time. —*Defn. 1. Oxford American Dictionary*

clairvoyance: (pg. 4) the supposed ability to perceive things that are not in sight or that cannot be seen. —*Defn. 1. Webster's New World Dictionary*

cleavage: (pg. 97) the state of being cleft (split; divided). —*Defn. 2. Random House College Dictionary*

combat fatigue: (pg. 99) a mental disorder due to stress in wartime combat. —*Oxford American Dictionary*

common denominator: (pg. 4) a trait, characteristic, belief or the like, common to or shared by all members of a group. —*Defn. 2. Random House College Dictionary*

company (military): (pg. 19) any relatively small group of soldiers. —*Defn. 9b. Random House College Dictionary*

complexion: (pg. 37) general appearance or nature; character; aspect. —*Defn. 3. Webster's New World Dictionary*

113

compulsion(s): (pg. 2) an irresistible, repeated, irrational impulse to perform some act. —*Defn. 3. Webster's New World Dictionary*

conception: (pg. 31) a conceiving (to become pregnant with; cause to begin life in the womb) or being conceived in the womb. —*Defn. 1. Webster's New World Dictionary*

connective tissue: (pg. 82) tissue found throughout the body, serving to bind together and support other tissues and organs. —*Webster's New World Dictionary*

consolidate(-ting): (pg. 9) to make or become strong, stable, firmly established, etc. —*Defn. 2. Webster's New World Dictionary*

consort: (pg. 90) to keep company; associate. —*Defn. 1. Webster's New World Dictionary*

contagion: (pg. 74) communication or transfer from one to another. —*editor*

contemporary: (pg. 46) up-to-date. —*Defn. 2. Oxford American Dictionary*

convulsion: (pg. 102) a violent, involuntary contraction or spasm of the muscles. —*Defn. 1. Webster's New World Dictionary*

cosmic: (pg. 7) of the universe. —*Defn. 1. Oxford American Dictionary* cursory(-rily): (pg. 12) hastily, often superficially, done; performed rapidly with little attention to detail. —*Webster's New World Dictionary*

deism: (pg. 4) belief in the existence of a God on purely rational grounds without reliance on revelation or authority; especially, the 17th and 18th century doctrine that God created the world and its natural laws, but takes no further part in its functioning. —*Webster's New World Dictionary*

114   delineate(d): (pg. 1) to depict in words; describe. —*Defn. 3. Webster's New World Dictionary*

delusion(s): (pg. 47) implies belief in something that is contrary to fact or reality, resulting from deception, a misconception or a mental disorder. —*Webster's New World Dictionary*

denote: (pg. 8) be a sign of; indicate. —*Defn. 1. Webster's New World Dictionary*

derange: (pg. 11) to upset the arrangement, order or operation of; unsettle; disorder. —*Defn. 1. Webster's New World Dictionary*

despondency: (pg. 56) loss of courage or hope; dejection. —*Webster's New World Dictionary*

detriment: (pg. 69) loss, damage, disadvantage or injury. —*Defn. 1. Random House College Dictionary*

develop(ed): (pg. 39) to become known or apparent; be disclosed. —*Defn. 3. Webster's New World Dictionary*

diagnostic: (pg. 28) of or constituting a diagnosis (a careful examination and analysis of the facts in an attempt to understand or explain something). —*Defn. 1. Webster's New World Dictionary*

Dickens, Charles: (pg. 48) English novelist of the late 19th century noted for picturesque and extravagant characters in the lower economic strata of England at that time. —*editor*

differential: (pg. 49) a difference between comparable things. —*Defn. 6. Webster's Third New International Dictionary*

dire: (pg. 75) dreadful, terrible. —*Defn. 1. Oxford American Dictionary*

discount(ed): (pg. 44) to disregard partly or wholly. —*Defn. 1. Oxford American Dictionary*

disperse(-sion): (pg. 15) to scatter, to go or drive or send in different directions. —*Oxford American Dictionary*

divergence: (pg. 97) a becoming different in form or kind. —*Defn. 2. Webster's New World Dictionary*

115

dramatis personae: (pg. 50) the characters in a play or story. —*Defn. 1. American Heritage Dictionary* [Used here to refer to people present in the engrams of the aberree.]

dramatization(s): (pg. 22) to repeat in action what has happened to one in experience. That's a basic definition of it, but much more important, it's a replay now of something that happened then. It's being replayed out of its time and period.

dynamic: (pg. 1) relating to energy or physical force in motion. —*Defn. 1. Webster's New World Dictionary*

dynamic principle of existence: (pg. 1) is **Survive!** No behavior or activity has been found to exist without this principle. It is not new that life is surviving. It is new that life has as its entire dynamic urge *only* survival.

dynamics: (pg. viii) there could be said to be eight urges (drives, impulses) in life. These we call dynamics. These are motives or motivations.

eccentricity(-ties): (pg. 48) deviation from what is ordinary or customary, as in conduct or manner; oddity; unconventionality. —*Defn. 2. Webster's New World Dictionary*

Educational Dianetics: (pg. 11) contains the body of organized knowledge necessary to train minds to their optimum efficiency and to an optimum of skill and knowledge in the various branches of the works of man.

electron(s): (pg. 74) a particle of matter with a negative electric charge. —*Oxford American Dictionary*

elicit: (pg. 63) to draw out (information, a response, etc.). —*Oxford American Dictionary*

116　**embrace(d):** (pg. 1) to include; contain. —*Defn. 5. Webster's New World Dictionary*

E-Meter: Hubbard Electrometer. An electronic instrument for measuring mental state and change of state in individuals, as an aid to precision and speed in auditing. The E-Meter is not intended or effective for the diagnosis, treatment or prevention of any disease.

emote: (pg. 66) to give expression to emotion. —*Webster's Third New International Dictionary*

emphatic(ally): (pg. 52) . . . decidedly; decisively. —*Defn. 1. Oxford English Dictionary*

encephalograph: (pg. 62) electroencephalograph (an instrument for measuring and recording the electric activity of the brain). —*Defn. 2. Random House College Dictionary*

endeavor: (pg. vii) an earnest attempt or effort. —*Webster's New World Dictionary*

engram: (pg. 22) a mental image picture which is a recording of a time of physical pain and unconsciousness. It must by definition have impact or injury as part of its content.

enjoin(ed): (pg. 59) to urge or impose with authority; order; enforce. —*Defn. 1. Webster's New World Dictionary*

equivocal: (pg. 36) uncertain; undecided; doubtful. —*Defn. 2. Webster's New World Dictionary*

erasure: (pg. 39) when applied to an engram which has been treated means that the engram has disappeared from the engram bank; it cannot be found afterwards except by search of the standard memory.

eugenic: (pg. 74) pertaining or adapted to the production of fine offspring especially in the human race. —*Defn. A. Oxford English Dictionary*

exhaust(ion): (pg. 29) to draw out or drain off completely. —*Defn. 6. Random House College Dictionary*

facet: (pg. 7) any of a number of sides or aspects, as of a personality. —*Defn. 2. Webster's New World Dictionary*

fetus: (pg. 31) in man, the offspring in the womb from the end of the third month of pregnancy until birth. —*Defn. 2. Webster's New World Dictionary*

flagrant: (pg. 48) very bad and obvious. —*Oxford American Dictionary*

flank: (pg. 65) the right or left side of a body of troops, etc. —*Defn. 3. Oxford American Dictionary*

forebear(s): (pg. 7) an ancestor. —*Webster's New World Dictionary*

forgetter: (pg. 45) any engram command which makes the individual believe he can't remember.

frontal lobe: (pg. 7) portion of the brain behind the forehead. —*editor*

genetic: (pg. 82) applies to the . . . line of father and mother to child, grown child to new child and so forth.

geometrical progression: (pg. 49) progression with a constant ratio between successive quantities, as 1:3:9:27:81. —*Oxford American Dictionary*

germane: (pg. 73) truly relevant; pertinent; to the point. —*Defn. 1. Webster's New World Dictionary*

glandular: (pg. 11) derived from or affected by glands [organs that secrete substances to be used in other parts of the body or expelled from it]. —*Defn. 3. Webster's New World Dictionary*

glean(s): (pg. 62) to collect or gather anything little by little or slowly. —*Defn. 3. Random House College Dictionary*

guile: (pg. 66) slyness and cunning in dealing with others; craftiness. —*Webster's New World Dictionary*

118

heuristic(ally): (pg. 1) serving to find out; specifically applied to a system of education under which the student is trained to find out things for himself. —*Defn. 1. Oxford Universal Dictionary*

hitherto: (pg. 2) until this time. —*Oxford American Dictionary*

hormone: (pg. 30) a substance formed in some organ of the body . . . [glands] and carried by a body fluid to another organ or tissue, where it has a specific effect. —*Defn. 1. Webster's New World Dictionary*

hypertension: (pg. 99) abnormally high blood pressure, or a disease of which this is the chief sign. —*Defn. 2. Webster's New World Dictionary*

hypnotic: (pg. 24) tending to produce sleep or a trance. —*editor*

hysteria(s): (pg. 44) any outbreak of wild, uncontrolled excitement or feeling, such as fits of laughing and crying. —*Defn. 2. Webster's New World Dictionary*

idealism: (pg. 3) behavior or thought based on a conception of things as they should be or as one would wish them to be. —*Defn. 1. Webster's New World Dictionary*

illusion(s): (pg. 47) suggests the false perception or interpretation of something that has objective existence. —*Webster's New World Dictionary*

impediment: (pg. 25) early term which meant the same as engram. —*editor*

implant(ed): (pg. 25) to plant firmly or deeply; embed. —*Defn. 1. Webster's New World Dictionary*

implicit: (pg. 94) without reservation or doubt; unquestioning; absolute. —*Defn. 3. Webster's New World Dictionary*

119

impunity: (pg. 90) exemption from punishment, penalty or harm. —*Webster's New World Dictionary*

inanimate: (pg. 6) (of rocks and other objects) lifeless, (of plants) lacking animal life. —*Defn. 1. Oxford American Dictionary*

indiscriminate: (pg. 43) not discriminating (to recognize the difference between); not making careful choices or distinctions. —*Defn. 2. Webster's New World Dictionary*

infatuate(-tion): (pg. 56) to inspire with foolish or shallow love or affection. —*Defn. 2. Webster's New World Dictionary*

inherent: (pg. 47) existing in something as a natural or permanent characteristic or quality. —*Oxford American Dictionary*

innate: (pg. 45) existing naturally rather than acquired; that seems to have been in one from birth. —*Defn. 1a. Webster's New World Dictionary*

innocuous: (pg. 91) that does not injure or harm; harmless. —*Defn. 1. Webster's New World Dictionary*

instinct: (pg. 13) an inborn impulse or tendency to perform certain acts or behave in certain ways. —*Defn. 1. Oxford American Dictionary*

insulin shock: (pg. 36) a state of collapse caused by a decrease in blood sugar resulting from the administration of excessive insulin. —*Random House College Dictionary*

integration: (pg. 21) the organization of various traits, feelings, attitudes, etc., into one harmonious personality. —*Defn. 3. Webster's New World Dictionary*

intersperse(d): (pg. 50) to scatter among other things; put here and there or at intervals. —*Defn. 1. Webster's New World Dictionary*

120   **intimidate(d):** (pg. 56) to make timid; make afraid. —*Defn. 1. Webster's New World Dictionary*

Judicial Dianetics: (pg. 11) covers the field of adjudication within the society and amongst the societies of man. Of necessity it embraces jurisprudence [science or philosophy of law] and its codes and establishes precision definitions and equations for the establishment of equity. It is the science of judgment.

key(s): (pg. 25) something that secures or controls entrance to a place. —*Defn. 6. Random House Dictionary of the English Language*

keynote: (pg. 18) the basic idea or ruling principle, as of a speech, policy, etc. —*Defn. 2. Webster's New World Dictionary*

kingdom(s): (pg. 4) any of the three great divisions into which all natural objects have been classified (the animal, vegetable and mineral kingdoms). —*Defn. 3. Webster's New World Dictionary*

libido(s): (pg. 33) the sexual urge or instinct. —*Defn. 1. Webster's New World Dictionary*

lift(ed): (pg. 66) to rise and vanish; be dispelled. —*Defn. 2. Webster's New World Dictionary*

lock(s): (pg. 28) an analytical moment in which the perceptics of the engram are approximated, thus restimulating the engram or bringing it into action, the present-time perceptics being erroneously interpreted by the reactive mind to mean that the same condition which produced physical pain once before is now again at hand.

Logics: (pg. 149) methods of thinking.

maladjustment: (pg. 33) lack of harmony between the individual and his environment. —*Defn. c. Webster's Third New International Dictionary*

manic: (pg. 51) a person exhibiting excessive or unreasonable enthusiasm. —*editor*

manifestation(s): (pg. 11) something that manifests or is manifested (to make clear or evident; show plainly; reveal). —*Defn. 2. Webster's New World Dictionary*

mind: (pg. 5) is the command post of operation and is constructed to resolve problems and pose problems related to survival and only to survival.

ministration(s): (pg. 85) the act or an instance of giving help or care; service. —*Defn. 2. Webster's New World Dictionary*

mutation: (pg. 5) change or alteration in form. —*Defn. 1. Oxford American Dictionary*

myopic: (pg. 99) nearsighted (seeing distinctly at a short distance only). —*Random House College Dictionary*

narcosynthesis: (pg. 59) the practice of inducing sleep with drugs and then talking to the patient to draw out buried thoughts.

natural selection: (pg. 5) a process in nature resulting in the survival and perpetuation of only those forms of plant and animal life having certain favorable characteristics that best enable them to adapt to a specific environment. —*Random House College Dictionary*

nebulous: (pg. 1) unclear; vague; indefinite. —*Defn. 3. Webster's New World Dictionary*

121

neurasthenia: (pg. 79) a type of neurosis . . . characterized by irritability, fatigue, weakness, anxiety and, often, localized pains or distress without apparent physical causes: formerly thought to result from weakness or exhaustion of the nervous system. —*Webster's New World Dictionary*

neurosis(-ses): (pg. 2) an emotional state containing conflicts and emotional data inhibiting the abilities or welfare of the individual.

nitrous oxide: (pg. 27) a colorless, nonflammable gas . . . used as an anesthetic and in aerosols. —*Webster's New World Dictionary*

122

noble: (pg. 55) very good or excellent; superior of its kind. —*Defn. 3b. Webster's Third New International Dictionary*

obstetrician(s): (pg. 86) a medical doctor who specializes in obstetrics (the branch of medicine concerned with the care and treatment of women during pregnancy, childbirth and the period immediately following). —*Webster's New World Dictionary*

obtain(s): (pg. 30) to be in force or in effect; prevail. —*Defn. 1. Webster's New World Dictionary*

occasion(ed): (pg. 15) to cause. —*Oxford American Dictionary*

olfactory: (pg. 24) of or pertaining to the sense of smell. —*Defn. 1. Random House College Dictionary*

pathological(ly): (pg. 33) due to or involving disease. —*Defn. 2. Webster's New World Dictionary*

patter: (pg. 74) special language or jargon. —*editor*

perceptics: (pg. 23) sense messages.

philosophy: (pg. 1) the rational investigation of the truths and principles of being, knowledge or conduct. —*Defn. 1. Random House College Dictionary*

phraseology: (pg. 47) choice and pattern of words; way of speaking or writing. —*Webster's New World Dictionary*

physio: (pg. 12) *a combining form meaning* physical. —*Defn. 2. Webster's New World Dictionary*

physiological(ly): (pg. 18) of or pertaining to physiology (the organic processes or functions of an organism or any of its parts). —*Defn. 1. Random House College Dictionary*

pitch: (pg. 23) that quality of a tone or sound determined by the frequency of vibration of the sound waves reaching the ear: the greater the frequency, the higher the pitch. —*Defn. 16a. Webster's New World Dictionary*

123

Political Dianetics: (pg. 11) embraces the field of group activity and organization to establish the optimum conditions and processes of leadership and intergroup relations.

pose(s): (pg. 6) to put forward, to present. —*Defn. 4. Oxford American Dictionary*

positive suggestion: (pg. 30) suggestion by the operator to a hypnotized subject with the sole end of creating a changed mental condition in the subject by implantation of the suggestion alone. It is the transplantation of something in the hypnotist's mind into the patient's mind. The patient is then to believe it and take it as part of himself.

posthypnotic: (pg. 30) of, having to do with or carried out in the period following a hypnotic trance. —*Webster's New World Dictionary*

precarious(ly): (pg. 32) dependent on chance circumstances, unknown conditions or uncertain developments; uncertain. —*Defn. 4a. Webster's Third New International Dictionary*

preclear: (pg. 20) any person who has been entered into Dianetics processing.

precursor(s): (pg. 27) earlier engram.

predominate(-ting): (pg. 95) to be the stronger or leading element; prevail. *—Defn. 1. Random House College Dictionary*

prefrontal lobotomy(-mies): (pg. 36) uses a scalpel or ice pick to perform an operation on the prefrontal lobes of the brain.

prejudicial: (pg. 44) tending to injure or impair. *—Defn. 1. Webster's Third New International Dictionary*

prenatal: (pg. 31) existing or taking place before birth. *—Webster's New World Dictionary*

124

prevalence: (pg. 83) widespread; of wide extent or occurrence; in general use or acceptance. *—Defn. 1. Random House Dictionary of the English Language*

procreate(-tion): (pg. 5) to bring (a living thing) into existence by the natural process of reproduction, to generate. *—Oxford American Dictionary*

progeny: (pg. 8) children, descendants or offspring collectively. *—Webster's New World Dictionary*

promiscuous(-cuity): (pg. 74) having sexual relations with many people. *—Defn. 2. Oxford American Dictionary*

proviso: (pg. 14) a condition or stipulation. *—Defn. 2. Webster's New World Dictionary*

psyche: (pg. 32) the human soul. *—Defn. 1. Webster's New World Dictionary*

psychic: (pg. 14) of or having to do with the psyche [soul] or mind. *—Defn. 1. Webster's New World Dictionary*

psychoanalysis: (pg. 90) method of mental therapy developed by Sigmund Freud in 1894. *—editor*

psychoneurotic: (pg. 76) neurotic: a person who is mainly harmful to himself by reason of his aberrations, but not to the point of suicide.

psychosis(-ses): (pg. 2) a conflict of commands which seriously reduce the individual's ability to solve his problems in his environment to a point where he cannot adjust some vital phase of his environmental needs.

psychosomatic: (pg. 2) *psycho* of course refers to mind and *somatic* refers to body; the term *psychosomatic* means the mind making the body ill or illnesses which have been created physically within the body by derangement of the mind.

pusillanimity: (pg. 21) lacking courage; cowardly. —*editor*

rationalize: (pg. 18) to explain or interpret on rational grounds. —*Defn. 2. Webster's New World Dictionary*

rave(-ing): (pg. 64) to talk wildly or furiously, to talk nonsensically in delirium; *raving mad,* completely mad. —*Defn. 1. Oxford American Dictionary*

reactive: (pg. 27) irrational, reacting instead of acting.

reactive mind: (pg. 2) the portion of the mind which works on a stimulus-response basis (given a certain stimulus it will automatically give a certain response) which is not under a person's volitional [of or having to do with a person's own power of choice] control and which exerts force and power over a person's awareness, purposes, thoughts, body and actions.

reactive thought: (pg. 9) the reactive mind is distinguished by the fact that although it thinks, it thinks wholly in identities. For instance, to the reactive mind under certain conditions there would be no difference between a microphone and a table.

rebuff(ed): (pg. 57) a blunt or abrupt rejection, as of a person's advances. —*Defn. 1. Random House College Dictionary*

regress(ed): (pg. 27) to go back; return; move backward. —*Defn. 1. Webster's New World Dictionary*

regression: (pg. 41) was a technique by which part of the individual's self remained in the present and part went back to the past. These abilities of the mind were supposed native only in hypnotism and were used only in hypnotic techniques.

reiterate(d): (pg. 68) to repeat (something done or said); say or do again or repeatedly. —*Webster's New World Dictionary*

Release: (pg. 34) an individual from whom mental stress and anxiety have been removed by Dianetics therapy.

repression(s): (pg. 2) a command that the organism must not do something.

126

resilient: (pg. 81) recovering readily from illness, depression, adversity or the like. —*Defn. 3. Random House College Dictionary*

resolve: (pg. 20) to determine or decide upon (a course of action, etc.). —*Defn. 14. Oxford English Dictionary*

retire: (pg. 18) to return; to come back. —*Defn. 4. Oxford English Dictionary*

returning: (pg. 59) the person can "send" a portion of his mind to a past period on either a mental or combined mental and physical basis and can reexperience incidents which have taken place in his past in the same fashion and with the same sensations as before.

reverie: (pg. 65) in reverie the preclear is placed in a light state of "concentration" which is not to be confused with hypnosis. The mind of the preclear will be found to be to some degree detachable from his surroundings and directed interiorly.

reverse(s): (pg. 43) a change from good fortune to bad; defeat. —*Defn. 4. Webster's New World Dictionary*

revivify: (pg. 52) relive.

sag: (pg. 52) to lose firmness, strength or intensity; weaken through weariness, age, etc.; droop. —*Defn. 3. Webster's New World Dictionary*

school: (pg. 3) a group of people held together by the same teachings, beliefs, opinions, methods, etc. . . . —*Defn. 8a. Webster's New World Dictionary*

Scientology: (pg. 145) Scientology® applied religious philosophy, the study of the human spirit in its relationship to the physical universe and its living forms. Note: Dianetics is the forerunner of Scientology and is in extensive use by Scientology churches and organizations all over the world.

scrutiny: (pg. 59) a close examination; minute inspection. —*Defn. 1. Webster's New World Dictionary*

secondary engram(s): (pg. 72) painful emotion engram, similar to other engrams, it is caused by the shock of sudden loss such as the death of a loved one.

self-determinism: (pg. 13) means the ability to direct oneself.

semantic: (pg. 3) of or pertaining to meaning, especially meaning in language. —*Defn. 1. Webster's New World Dictionary*

semantics: (pg. 23) the study of meaning. —*Defn. 1a. Random House College Dictionary*

sensory strip: (pg. 61) the sensory strip could be considered the mental side of the switchboard and the motor strip the physical side.

sentient: (pg. 86) of, having or capable of feeling or perception; conscious. —*Webster's New World Dictionary*

somatic: (pg. 27) body sensation, illness or pain or discomfort. "Soma" means body. Hence psychosomatic or pains stemming from the mind.

somnambulism(-stic): (pg. 13) the trancelike state of one who somnambulates (to get up and move about in a trancelike state while asleep). —*Webster's New World Dictionary*

sporadic: (pg. 35) happening from time to time; not constant or regular; occasional. —*Defn. 1. Webster's New World Dictionary*

static: (pg. 97) not changing. —*Defn. 3. Oxford American Dictionary*

subbrains: (pg. 12) there is a subbrain in various parts of the body . . . such parts of the body as the "funny bones" or any "judo sensitive" spots: the sides of the neck, the inside of the wrist, the places the doctors tap to find out if there is a reflex.

succumb: (pg. 43) to give way (to); yield; submit. —*Defn. 1. Webster's New World Dictionary*

superimpose(d): (pg. 7) to lay or place (a thing) on top of something else. —*Oxford American Dictionary*

supplant(s): (pg. 24) to take the place of; supersede, especially through force or plotting. —*Defn. 1. Webster's New World Dictionary*

surcharge: (pg. 26) an overcharge. —*Defn. 1b. Webster's New World Dictionary*

sustenance: (pg. 82) the food itself, nourishment. —*Defn. 2. Oxford American Dictionary*

syllabic: (pg. 23) of a syllable or syllables. —*Defn. 1. Webster's New World Dictionary*

symbiote(s): (pg. 6) the Dianetics meaning of *symbiote* is extended beyond the dictionary definition to mean "any or all life or energy forms which are mutually dependent for survival." The atom depends on the universe, the universe on the atom.

sympathetic: (pg. 51) showing favor, approval or agreement. —*Defn. 3. Webster's New World Dictionary*

sympathy engram: (pg. 64) an engram of a very specific nature, being the effort of the parent or guardian to be kind to a child who is severely hurt.

tactile: (pg. 24) of, having or related to the sense of touch. —*Defn. 2. Webster's New World Dictionary*

tantrum(s): (pg. 44) a violent, willful outburst of annoyance, rage, etc.; childish fit of bad temper. —*Webster's New World Dictionary*

telepathy: (pg. 4) communication from one mind to another without the use of speech or writing or gestures, etc. —*Oxford American Dictionary*

tenacity: (pg. 7) the quality or state of being tenacious (persistent; stubborn). —*Webster's New World Dictionary*

129

timbre: (pg. 23) the characteristic quality of sound that distinguishes one voice or musical instrument from another or one vowel sound from another: it is determined by the harmonics of the sound and is distinguished from the intensity and pitch. —*Webster's New World Dictionary*

time track: (pg. 13) consists of all the consecutive moments of *now* from the earliest moment of life of the organism to present time.

tone scale: (pg. viii) is essentially an assignation of numerical value by which individuals can be numerically classified. It is not arbitrary but will be found to approximate some actual governing law in nature.

trance: (pg. 27) to put in a trance (a half-conscious state, seemingly between sleeping and waking, in which ability to function voluntarily may be suspended). —*Defn. 6. Random House College Dictionary*

trite: (pg. 62) worn out by constant use; no longer having freshness, originality or novelty; stale. —*Webster's New World Dictionary*

tuberculosis: (pg. 99) an infectious disease that may affect almost any tissue of the body, especially the lungs. —*Random House College Dictionary*

tyranny(-nies): (pg. 99) oppressive, severe and unjust domination. —*Defn. 3a. Webster's Third New International Dictionary*

umbilical cord: (pg. 85) cord connected to the navel of the fetus to supply nourishment prior to birth. —*editor*

vice(s): (pg. 22) an evil or wicked action, habit or characteristic. —*Defn. 1a. Webster's New World Dictionary*

virtue(s): (pg. 21) moral excellence, goodness, a particular form of this. —*Defn. 1. Oxford American Dictionary*

visio: (pg. 23) with visio we perceive light waves, which, as sight, are compared with experience and evaluated.

130

weight: (pg. 18) influence, power or authority. —*Defn. 8. Webster's New World Dictionary*

Index

analytical mind, *(cont.)*
is variable, 7–8
lock can be reached by, 28
must never permit an incorrect
solution, 43
only way to aberrate, 45
paralyzed by hypnotic drugs, 60
protected by fuse system, 15
reaction to reactive mind, 43, 48, 92
reduction of awareness potential of, 24,
49, 51
relation to restimulation and tone level,
35–36, 43–44
restoration of ability of, 35–36
superimposed on brain, 7
whatever contests the, 63

analytical power, 32

analyzer, 33, 41; *see also* analytical mind

anesthetics, 60

antagonistic, 27

antipathies, 46

"appreciator," 43

artistry, 22

"assist engram," 51–52

asthma, 86

astigmatism, myopic, 99

attempted abortion(s); *see also*
prenatal engram(s)
are common, 66
auditor should suspect in every case, 83
damage to fetus by, 82
disbelief of, 67
discovery of, 83
dramatization of, in society, 84
engram containing, 48
example of, 101
indicators of, 67, 68, 83
is usual basic, 67
most serious aberration producer, 83
relation to criminal, 83
unconsciousness from, 85
when only prenatal is, 66

audio-perceptics, 23

**audio-syllabic communications
system,** 23

auditing, 59–62; *see also* technique
basic principles of, 45
consists of, 59
difficulties in, 95, 96
irrational response to, 48
simplest form applied, 60
understanding the principles of, 68

auditor(s),
antagonism toward, 63, 71, 94
approach to case by, 66
biggest problem of, 68
cooperation with, 94
dynamics of, 92–93
encountering phrases in engrams, 85
failure to follow code, 55
functions as extra analytical mind, 59
gleans data from preclear, 62
handling of married preclear, 75–76
handling of prenatal area, 83–84
must be cleared, 55, 90
must think way through every case, 68–69
occasionally necessary to change, 93–94
primary task of, 61
problems of cases and, 74
purpose of, 45
purpose of preclear and, 73–74
recognition of phrases by, 91
restimulation of, 55
should be prepared to audit whole family
of preclear, 76
should find earliest chain, 77
sole interest of, 94
technique and, 92
understanding of principles and
definitions, 22, 77
use of engramic thought by, 42, 68

Auditor's Code, 55–57, 94

auto-control, 45–46

awareness, 51

axioms, primary, 3–9

basic (engram); *see also* chain
attempted abortion as, 101
attempt to reach, 94–95
case entry and, 80
defined, 77

135

137

139

141

Bibliography

More books by L. Ron Hubbard

All the following books by L. Ron Hubbard can be obtained from the publisher or any Scientology[1] church or organization listed in the back of this book.

Dianetics: The Modern Science of Mental Health

In *Dianetics*, you'll learn all about the Reactive Mind, what it does to you, and most important, how you can control it and bring out a strong, self-confident you. *Dianetics* has sold over 5 million copies. And for one reason: it works. Available at bookstores everywhere.

Dianetics: The Evolution of a Science

Written with brilliance and enthusiasm. *Evolution of a Science* tells the story of L. Ron Hubbard's research into the subject of *Dianetics*™ spiritual healing technology, a subject that has helped millions to gain trust and confidence in themselves. If you're interested in how Dianetics technology came about and what it can do for you and the goals in life you've always had, this book is for you.

Notes on the Lectures

In the rush of excitement immediately following the release of *Dianetics: The Modern Science of Mental Health*, Ron was in demand all over the country as a speaker. He has delivered over

---

1. Scientology: Scientology® applied religious philosophy, the study of the human spirit in its relationship to the physical universe and its living forms. Note: Dianetics is the forerunner of Scientology and is in extensive use by Scientology churches and organizations all over the world.

3,000 hours of lectures. This book is compiled from lectures given in the fall of 1950. Ron expands upon aspects of Dianetics processing and application of Dianetics principles to groups.

Child Dianetics

Have you all but given up on handling children? Parents who read *Child Dianetics* and apply its simple exercises to their children will find out something can be done!

146

Science of Survival

This book is built around a chart, The Chart of Human Evaluation. *Science of Survival* is a huge volume packed with information to help you deal successfully with other people and improve interpersonal and business relationships.

Self Analysis

Self Analysis is a simple, self-help volume designed for use a few minutes each day, by anyone. Use *Self Analysis* to unlock a stronger more confident "you" simply by reliving past pleasures you've enjoyed. A proven system that's so easy you won't believe it works—until you try it. Available at bookstores everywhere.

Advanced Procedures and Axioms

Advanced Dianetics discoveries and techniques. In this book L. Ron Hubbard details the types of cases an auditor will handle and advanced processes for handling these cases.

Dianetics 55!

In this book, L. Ron Hubbard deals with the problems and fundamental principles of communication between man and man, and between man and his environment.

Have You Lived Before This Life?

Many professionals today have stated that men may have lived in past lives. But, is this really true? Now, trained Scientologists have tested a series of forty-one cases. Their fascinating findings are given in this book.

The Basic Dianetics Picture Book

A visual aid for a quicker understanding and explanation of Dianetics and Dianetics processing.

147

Dianetics Today

Published in 1975, this book details the developments by L. Ron Hubbard in Dianetics technology twenty-five years after *Dianetics: The Modern Science of Mental Health* was first released.

Research and Discovery Series: Volumes 1–4

There are about 25 million words of taped lectures which contain the consecutive path of discovery made by L. Ron Hubbard. These lectures are being transcribed, compiled and published as the *Research and Discovery Series*. The first four volumes of this large series (75–100 volumes) covering the research and development of Dianetics and Scientology are now available. Fundamental, vital information, basic in Dianetics technology, demonstration sessions of Dianetics auditing and data on what Ron was doing in these first months of the development of Dianetics, all make these books fascinating and informative reading. These books contain information about Dianetics techniques never before published.

Handbook for Preclears

For use as a self-help volume or to apply to others, this book is designed to increase personal ability, efficiency and overall well-being.

A History of Man

A list and description of the principal incidents to be found on the time track of a human being. "This is a cold-blooded and factual account of your last sixty trillion years."

Scientology 8-80

The discovery and increase of life energy in Homo sapiens. This book will give you a real understanding of how energy relates to you.

Scientology 8-8008

In this book L. Ron Hubbard describes processes designed to increase the abilities of man as a spiritual being to heights only dreamed of before now.

The Creation of Human Ability

A huge number of processes for use by Scientology auditors, with full illumination of the major philosophical and technical breakthroughs by L. Ron Hubbard from which the techniques were derived.

Scientology: The Fundamentals of Thought

Contains basic data on handling life that will satisfy any seeker of workable knowledge. Here is the first book a person should read as an introduction to Scientology philosophy.

The Problems of Work

In these days of high unemployment and uncertain economies, you need to have every possible edge to get and *keep* jobs. This volume has just that. Invaluable knowledge of how to increase your efficiency and value on today's job market.

All About Radiation

Bluntly informative. A vital application of Scientology. Observations and discoveries concerning the mental aspects of radiation and their handling. A very important volume in today's world of nuclear power plants and concern about nuclear weapons.

Control and the Mechanics of Start-Change-Stop

Edited from the tape lectures of L. Ron Hubbard. This book covers various aspects and manifestations of the subject of control.

Scientology: Clear Procedure

This booklet gives processes to bring preclears to the state of Clear, a state of sanity and well-being never before achieved by man.

Axioms and Logics[2]

This book gives the basics of Dianetics and Scientology techniques and philosophy.

The Book of Case Remedies

The trained auditor's and student's manual covering preclear difficulties and their remedies. Loaded with brilliant case resolutions and notes by L. Ron Hubbard.

Scientology: A New Slant on Life

This is an introductory volume to Scientology applied religious philosophy. It gives invaluable information that applies to every aspect of life, from how to live with children to how to study sciences.

2.　Logics: methods of thinking.

The Phoenix Lectures

In July 1954, L. Ron Hubbard gave a series of lectures to students studying to become professional auditors. These lectures contained a tremendous amount of knowledge and were later published in book form. In these lectures L. Ron Hubbard discussed the general background of Scientology philosophy and gave a detailed explanation of many Scientology axioms. Fascinating reading.

Introduction to Scientology Ethics

Learn from this book the relationship of ethics to survival. Discover why people remain in unwanted conditions and what to do about it.

Scientology 0-8
The Book of Basics

This book contains fundamental information about the interrelationships of the different aspects of Scientology philosophy and techniques.

Background and Ceremonies of the Church of Scientology

The background and religious origins of the Church of Scientology, the Creed of the Church, church services, sermons, many ceremonies as originally given in person by L. Ron Hubbard, Founder of Scientology.

The Basic Scientology Picture Book Volume I

A visual aid to a better understanding of man and the material universe.

Mission into Time

This book is an account of L. Ron Hubbard's adventure into past lives and some of his thoughts and findings on the subject. Fascinating reading.

Hymn of Asia

Destined to be among the greatest of religious classics of mankind. Contains colorful and splendid artwork and photography.

The Technical Bulletins of Dianetics and Scientology

Twelve volumes, containing all of L. Ron Hubbard's technical bulletins and issues from 1950 to 1979. Every question a person may have concerning Dianetics and Scientology technology can be answered directly from the pages of these books, which also include a 250 page master subject index containing over 20,000 entries!

151

The Volunteer Minister's Handbook

Have you ever felt that you wanted to do something about the unhappiness, cruelty, injustice and violence of this society? Well now you can, with the materials included in this huge volume. This book is especially designed for people who want to learn how to help others. It is broken down into 21 sections, each covering an aspect of life. Anyone can become a Volunteer Minister and ably handle such situations as: broken marriages, accidents, drug or alcohol problems, a failing business, difficult children—just to name a few of the conditions that a Volunteer Minister can help to change.

What Is Scientology?

Here, at last, is a definitive collection of facts and figures, on and about what millions consider to be the most extraordinary phenomenon of our time. What is Scientology all about? Where is it headed? What makes it the fastest growing religion in the world today? The answers to these, and many other questions on the subject, are contained in this new book.

Philadelphia Doctorate Course Lectures

Lectures explaining the nature of spiritual beings and their relationship to the physical universe. These lectures, seventy-six in all, are recorded on high-quality cassette tapes. Transcripts of these lectures, available only with the cassettes, are also being released, each with a glossary and complete index.

The Way to Happiness

Man's first common-sense, nonreligious moral code. Twenty-one rules or statements of principles of conduct based on observation and knowledge of the nature of man. Buy it in packets of 12 booklets, read it and give it to your friends.

Introductory and Demonstration Processes and Assists[3]

Have you ever felt that there was something more you could do for an injured person than to call an ambulance? Ever been totally at a loss about what to do with a child having a temper tantrum? Well this pack of material has the answers to these and many other questions. There are a vast number of processes that L. Ron Hubbard developed that fall under the heading of Introductory, Assist and Demonstration processes. Many of these are in early Dianetics and Scientology publications or on taped lectures. A portion of these processes have been compiled in this pack so that they can be readily available for use. Contained in this pack are processes for children, processes to demonstrate Dianetics and Scientology, processes to help injured people and even processes that you can use on animals. Also given in this pack are the theory materials that apply to these processes.

How to Live Though an Executive

A must for any executive or anyone who works near one. Hundreds of applications in every phase of life. L. Ron Hubbard's earliest book on the subject of organization.

The Organization Executive Course

The Organization Executive Course volumes consist of eight large-format books containing L. Ron Hubbard's incredibly workable organizational technology. L. Ron Hubbard has said, "If

---

3.   assists: simple, easily done processes that can be applied to anyone to help them recover more rapidly from accidents, mild illness or upsets.

anyone knew the *Organization Executive Course* fully and could practice it, he could completely reverse any down-trending company or country." With the data contained in these volumes at your fingertips, you literally can handle any situation in a business, profession or any organization. How to survive in today's world of job scarcity, rising prices and material shortages is a question many people are asking. Practical answers and satisfying results await you when you use these volumes.

The Management Series

Almost every day in the news one can hear about the rising amount of business failures. These aren't just small businesses, but huge corporations, banks and even national economies. One could get the idea that the people running things were missing some basic, vital knowledge about how to manage. These books by L. Ron Hubbard have the knowledge that has been missing. L. Ron Hubbard covers all aspects of management in these volumes from evaluation of information to public relations and finance. No manager can afford to get along without these books.

The Policy Subject Index

An index of all organizational policy from the first right up to August of 1975. It lists all of these policies under likely titles. You don't have to know the exact title of a policy to find it, and you don't have to know the date. This book goes along with the *Organization Executive Course* volumes and *The Management Series*.

Modern Management Technology Defined
Hubbard Dictionary of Administration and Management

A comprehensive dictionary containing the entire range of business terminology, including such areas as personnel management, communication within the group, financial management and data evaluation. This book provides the key to new clarity and understanding in the field of management and defines all the terms one will encounter in the *Organization Executive Course* and the *Management Series*.

Dianetics and Scientology Technical Dictionary

Early schools of thought had no adequate technology or terminology. So as Ron developed Dianetics and Scientology, he also developed new terms to prevent confusions with other subjects that were not workable. This work defines the terminology of Dianetics and Scientology and makes it easy to clear up these new terms for someone else.

The Study Tapes

154

When you were in school did you ever ask your teacher what you actually were supposed to do when she told you to study something? The subject of study and the actual way to study has never been truly laid down before L. Ron Hubbard recorded these taped lectures. With these cassette lectures and transcript booklet you will learn how to *really* study and increase your skills in any field you wish to take up. Priceless in today's world with the ever increasing demand for new skills and skilled professionals.

Basic Dictionary of Dianetics and Scientology

A simple dictionary of terms, ideal for the new Scientologist or for explaining Scientology to your friends and relatives.

The worst part of you is hiding the best part

There's a part of your mind known as the *Reactive* Mind— and it's the worst enemy you have.

155

Your Reactive Mind is where all the hurts, heartbreaks, injuries and scares you've ever suffered are stored. Whenever you're unsure of yourself, nervous, angry or scared, it's not really you. It's your Reactive Mind stirring up past pains, making you do and feel things you shouldn't have to.

But now you can learn to control your Reactive Mind and all those things it makes you feel and do. It's all explained in *Dianetics:*™ *The Modern Science of Mental Health* by L. Ron Hubbard.

In it, you'll read all about your Reactive Mind, how it works, and most important, how you can learn to control it. *Dianetics* is one of the top best sellers of all time with over five million copies sold. And for a good reason: it works.

Underneath that Reactive Mind of yours, there's a strong, confident winner of a person. You can find that person with *Dianetics*.

Buy your copy of
Dianetics: The Modern Science of Mental Health.

Get it wherever paperbacks are sold, or order direct from the publisher, Bridge Publications, Inc., 1414 N. Catalina Street, Los Angeles, California 90027-9990.

What are the real capabilities of the mind?

How can we realize that potential?

It has been stated that Man uses only five to ten percent of his mental faculties. The full capabilities of the mind have never been measured.

Now you can learn how to discover your full, inherent potential with Dianetics™ spiritual healing technology.

In *Dianetics: The Evolution of a Science*, L. Ron Hubbard takes you on an exciting adventure—the discovery of *self*.

Explore, with Hubbard, the true, amazing potentials of the human mind. Discover the blocks and barriers in the mind that prevent that potential from being realized.

Most importantly, find out how you can use the breakthroughs of Dianetics to realize your own true capabilities and release the strong, confident winner within you.

Buy *Dianetics: The Evolution of a Science.*

Ask for it at your bookstore, or order direct from Bridge Publications, Inc., 1414 N. Catalina Street, Los Angeles, California 90027-9990.

Unlock a stronger, more confident "you"

Right now, all by yourself, you can do more to help   157
your well-being than you ever thought possible. All it takes is about
half an hour a day and *Self Analysis* by L. Ron Hubbard, the author
who has helped millions unlock their hidden potential.

A detailed Chart of Human Evaluation shows you where
your personal strengths and barriers are. Then you're ready to embark
on the processing section—a joyful and revealing journey of self-
discovery.

You'll rediscover pleasure-filled events such as recalling
when "you kissed somebody you liked . . . somebody was proud of
you . . . you stayed with your purpose . . ."

Many educators, therapists, artists and writers have used
Self Analysis and report astonishing results:

* More self-confidence
* A greater sense of well-being
* Improved memory
* Clearer thinking

Buy *Self Analysis* by L. Ron Hubbard.

Join the great adventure of *Self Analysis,* and in the words
of L. Ron Hubbard, "May you never be the same again." Read it.
Available at bookstores everywhere.

Address List

DIANETICS ® LOS GATOS
475 ALBERTO WAY SUITE 110
LOS GATOS, CA 95032
(408) 354-1201

158   ## How to Find a Dianetics Auditor

Skilled professional Dianetics auditors can be contacted at any of the following Churches of Scientology and Scientology organizations.

Dianetics is the forerunner of Scientology and is in extensive use by Scientology organizations and Churches throughout the world.

If you would like more information about Dianetics or how to process others with Dianetics, contact your nearest Church of Scientology or Scientology organization as listed below.

Western United States

Albuquerque
Church of Scientology of New Mexico
2712 Carlisle Boulevard N.E.
Albuquerque, New Mexico 87110

Austin
Church of Scientology of Texas
2200 Guadalupe
Austin, Texas 78705

Denver
Church of Scientology of Colorado
375 South Navajo Street
Denver, Colorado 80223

Honolulu
Church of Scientology of Hawaii
447 Nahua Street
Honolulu, Hawaii 96815

Kansas City
Church of Scientology of the Midwest
1206 West 39th Street
Kansas City, Missouri 64111

Las Vegas
Church of Scientology of Nevada
846 East Sahara Avenue
Las Vegas, Nevada 89104

Los Angeles

Church of Scientology of Los Angeles
4810 Sunset Boulevard
Los Angeles, California 90027

Minneapolis

Church of Scientology of Minnesota
900 Hennepin Avenue
Minneapolis, Minnesota 55403

Pasadena

Church of Scientology Pasadena
99 East Colorado Boulevard
Pasadena, California 91105

Phoenix

Church of Scientology of Arizona
4450 North Central Avenue, #102
Phoenix, Arizona 85012

Portland

Church of Scientology of Portland
215 South East 9th Avenue
Portland, Oregon 97214

Sacramento

Church of Scientology of Sacramento
825 15th Street
Sacramento, California 95814-2096

San Diego

Church of Scientology of San Diego
348 Olive Street
San Diego, California 92103

San Fernando Valley

Church of Scientology
San Fernando Valley
13561 Ventura Boulevard
Sherman Oaks, California 91403

San Francisco

Church of Scientology of San Francisco
83 McAllister Street
San Francisco, California 94102

Santa Barbara

Church of Scientology Santa Barbara
20 West De la Guerra
Santa Barbara, California 93101

Seattle

Church of Scientology of Washington State
222 Mercer Street
Seattle, Washington 98109

St. Louis

Church of Scientology of Missouri
3730 Lindell Boulevard
St. Louis, Missouri 63108

Eastern United States

Boston

Church of Scientology of Boston
448 Beacon Street
Boston, Massachusetts 02115

Buffalo

Church of Scientology Buffalo
47 West Huron Street
Buffalo, New York 14202

Chicago

Church of Scientology of Illinois
845 Chicago Avenue
Evanston, Illinois 60202

Cincinnati

Church of Scientology of Ohio
3352 Jefferson Avenue
Cincinnati, Ohio 45220

Columbus

Church of Scientology of Central Ohio
167 East State Street
Columbus, Ohio 43215

Detroit

Church of Scientology of Michigan
751 Griswold
Detroit, Michigan 48226

Long Island

Church of Scientology of Long Island
46 Islip Avenue
Islip, New York 11751

159

Miami

Church of Scientology of Florida
120 Giralda Avenue
Coral Gables, Florida 33134

New Haven

Church of Scientology of New Haven
909 Whalley Avenue
New Haven, Connecticut 06515

New York City

Church of Scientology of New York
227 West 46th Street
New York City, New York 10036

Orlando

Church of Scientology of Orlando
111 East Robinson Street
Orlando, Florida 32801

Philadelphia

Church of Scientology of Pennsylvania
1315–17 Race Street
Philadelphia, Pennsylvania 19107

Tampa

Church of Scientology of Tampa
436 West Kennedy Boulevard
Tampa, Florida 33606

Washington, D.C.

Founding Church of Scientology
2125 "S" Street N.W.
Washington, D.C. 20008

Canada

Edmonton

Church of Scientology of Alberta
10349 82nd Avenue
Edmonton, Alberta
Canada T6E 1Z9

Kitchener

Church of Scientology of Kitchener
8 Water Street North
Kitchener, Ontario
Canada N2H 5A5

Montreal

Church of Scientology of Montréal
4489 Papineau Street
Montréal, Québec
Canada H2H 1T7

Ottawa

Church of Scientology Ottawa
309 Cooper Street, 5th Floor
Ottawa, Ontario
Canada K2P 0G5

Quebec

Church of Scientology of Québec
224½ St-Joseph est
Québec, Québec
Canada G1K 3A9

Toronto

Church of Scientology of Toronto
696 Yonge Street
Toronto, Ontario
Canada M4Y 2A7

Vancouver

Church of Scientology of British Colombia
401 West Hastings Street
Vancouver, British Columbia
Canada V6B 1L5

Winnipeg

Church of Scientology of Winnipeg
689 St. Mary's Road
Winnipeg, Manitoba
Canada R2M 3M8

United Kingdom

Birmingham

Scientology Birmingham
3 St. Mary's Row
Moseley, Birmingham
England B13 8HW

Edinburgh

Hubbard Academy of Personal
Independence
20 Southbridge
Edinburgh, Scotland EH1 1LL

London

Church of Scientology in London
68 Tottenham Court Road
London, England W1E 4YZ

Manchester

Church of Scientology Manchester
258/260 Deansgate
Manchester, England M3 4BG

Plymouth

Church of Scientology in Plymouth
41 Ebrington Street
Plymouth, Devon
England PL4 9AA

Sunderland

Scientology Sunderland
211 High Street West
Sunderland, Tyne and Wear
England SR1 1UA

Austria

Church of Scientology Vienna
(Scientology-Österreich)
Mariahilferstrasse 88A/II/2
A-1070 Vienna, Austria

Belgium

Church of Scientology of Belgium
45A, Rue de l'Ecuyer
1000 Bruxelles, Belgium

Denmark

Århus

Church of Scientology Jylland
Søndergade 70, 1th
8000 Århus C., Denmark

Copenhagen

Church of Scientology Copenhagen
Store Kongensgade 55
1264 Copenhagen K, Denmark

Copenhagen

Church of Scientology Denmark
Vesterbrogade 23 A – 25
1620 Copenhagen V, Denmark

France

Angers

Church of Scientology Angers
10–12, rue Max Richard
49002 Angers Cedex, France

Clermont-Ferrand

Church of Scientology Clermont-Ferrand
18, rue André Moinier
63000 Clermont-Ferrand, France

Lyon

Church of Scientology Lyon
Chemin du Pont aux Biches
69250 Neuville/Saône, France

Paris

Church of Scientology of Paris
12, rue de la Montagne Sainte Geneviève
75005 Paris, France

St. Etienne

Church of Scientology St Etienne
10, rue de la Paix
42000 St Etienne, France

Germany

Berlin

Church of Scientology Berlin
HSO Berlin e.V.
Jagowstrasse 15
D-1000 Berlin 21, Germany

Munich

Church of Scientology München
Beichstrasse 12
D-8000 München 40, West Germany

Netherlands

Church of Scientology Amsterdam
Nieuwe Zijds Voorburgwal 312
1012 RV Amsterdam, Netherlands

Norway

Church of Scientology Oslo
Stenersgaten 16
Oslo 1, Norway

162

Sweden

Göteborg

Church of Scientology Göteborg
Kungsgatan 23
S-411 19 Göteborg, Sweden

Malmö

Church of Scientology Malmö
Stortorget 27-29
S-211 34 Malmö, Sweden

Stockholm

Church of Scientology Stockholm
Kammakargatan 46
S-111 60 Stockholm, Sweden

Switzerland

Basel

Church of Scientology Basel
Gundeldingerstrasse 432
4053 Basel, Switzerland

Bern

Church of Scientology Bern
Effingerstrasse 25
3008 Bern, Switzerland

Geneva

Church of Scientology Genève
4, rue du Léman
1201 Genève, Switzerland

Australia and New Zealand

Adelaide

Church of Scientology Adelaide
28 Waymouth Street
Adelaide, South Australia 5000
Australia

Auckland

Church of Scientology of New Zealand
44 Queen Street, 2nd Floor
Auckland 1, New Zealand

Brisbane

Church of Scientology Brisbane
64 Tait Street
Kelvin Grove
Brisbane, Queensland 4059
Australia

Canberra

Church of Scientology A.C.T.
23 East Row, Rooms 2&3
Civic, Canberra
A.C.T. 2601
Australia

Melbourne

Church of Scientology Melbourne
42 Russell Street
Melbourne, Victoria 3000
Australia

Perth

Church of Scientology Perth
3rd Floor, Pastoral House
156 St. George's Terrace
Perth, Western Australia 6000
Australia

Sydney

Church of Scientology Sydney
201 Castlereagh Street
Sydney, New South Wales 2000
Australia

Africa

Bulawayo
Church of Scientology in Zimbabwe
74 Abercorn Street
Bulawayo, Zimbabwe/Rhodesia

Cape Town
Church of Scientology in South Africa
3rd Floor, Garmor House
127 Plein Street
Cape Town 8001, South Africa

Durban
Church of Scientology in South Africa
57 College Lane
Durban 4001, South Africa

Harare/Salisbury
Church of Scientology Harare
102 Barton House
Corner Stanley Avenue & Moffat Street
Harare, Zimbabwe/Rhodesia

Johannesburg
Church of Scientology in South Africa
Security Building, 2nd Floor
95 Commissioner Street
Johannesburg 2001, South Africa

Church of Scientology Johannesburg North
207–210 Ivylink, 124 Ivy Road/Weg
Norwood 2192
Johannesburg, South Africa

Port Elizabeth
Church of Scientology Port Elizabeth
2 St. Christopher Place
27 Westbourne Road
Port Elizabeth 6001, South Africa

Pretoria
Church of Scientology in South Africa
226 Central House
Central Street
Pretoria 0002, South Africa

Latin America

Bogota
Centro Cultural de Dianética
Carrera 13 No. 90–36
Apartado Aereo 92419
Bogota, D.E. Colombia

Estado de Mexico
Instituto Tecnologico de Dianética, A.C.
Circunvalacion Poniente 150
Zona Azul Ciudad Satelite
53100 Estado de México, México

Mexico City
Asociación Cultural Dianética, A.C.
Hermes No. 46
Colonia Crédito Constructor
03940 México 19, D.F.

Instituto de Filosofia Aplicada, A.C.
Havre Numero 32
Colonia Juárez
06600 México 6, D.F.

Instituto de Filosofia Aplicada, A.C.
Plaza Rio de Janeiro 52
Colonia Roma
06700 México 7, D.F.

Organizacion Desarrollo y Dianética, A.C.
Providencia 1000
Colonia Del Valle
03100 México 12, D.F.

Centro de Dianética de Polanco, A.C.
Mariano Escobedo 524
Colonia Anzures
11590 México D.F.

Valencia
Associación Cultural de Dianética, A.C.
Calle 150 No. 100–223
Apartado Postal 711
Valencia, Venezuela

Greece
Hubbard Dianetics Institute
Ippokratous Street 175B
Athens, Greece

163

Israel

Scientology Israel
Scientology *"Shalom"* Center
6 Frishman Street
Tel Aviv 63 578, Israel

Italy

Brescia

Dianetics Institute Brescia
Via Einaudi 11/B
25100 Brescia, Italy

Milan

Dianetics Institute di Milano
Galleria del Corso 4
20122 Milano, Italy

Novara

Dianetics Institute Novara
Via Rosselli 10
28100 Novara, Italy

Padua

Associazione di Dianetics e Scientology
Padova
Via Pietro d'Abano 1
35100 Padova, Italy

Pordenone

Associazione di Dianetics e Scientology
Pordenone
Viale Martelli 4
33170 Pordenone, Italy

Rome

Associazione di Dianetics e Scientology di
Roma
Via Francesco Carrara 24
00196 Roma, Italy

Turin

Dianetics Institute Torino
Piazza Carlo Felice 80
10121 Torino, Italy

Verona

Associazione di Dianetics e Scientology
Verona
Via Leoncino 36
37121 Verona, Italy

Portugal

Instituto de Dianética Lisboa
Travessa Da Trindade 12–4
1200 Lisboa, Portugal

Spain

Barcelona

Asociación civil de Dianética
Calle Puertaferrisa *17 (2º Piso)*
Barcelona 2, Spain

Madrid

Asociación civil de Dianética
Montera 20
Madrid 14, Spain

Celebrity Centres

Ann Arbor

Church of Scientology
Celebrity Centre of Ann Arbor
301 North Ingalls
Ann Arbor, Michigan 48104

Las Vegas

Church of Scientology
Celebrity Centre Las Vegas
3430 E. Tropicana, Suite 50
Las Vegas, Nevada 89121

Los Angeles

Church of Scientology
Celebrity Centre Los Angeles
5930 Franklin Avenue
Hollywood, California 90028

Paris

Church of Scientology
Celebrity Centre Paris
41, rue de la Tour d'Auvergne
75009 Paris, France